W. Kirk MacNulty

Freemasonry

A Journey through Ritual and Symbol

with 133 illustrations, 17 in color

Thames and Hudson

For Christine

ART AND IMAGINATION

Any copy of this book issued by the publisher
as a paperback is sold subject to the
condition that it shall not by way of trade or
otherwise be lent, resold, hired out or
otherwise circulated without the publisher's
prior consent in any form of binding or cover
other than that in which it is published and
without a similar condition including these
words being imposed on a subsequent
purchaser.

© 1991 Thames and Hudson Ltd, London

First published in the United States in 1991 by
Thames and Hudson Inc., 500 Fifth Avenue,
New York, New York 10110

Library of Congress Catalog Card Number
91–65320

All Rights Reserved. No part of this publication
may be reproduced or transmitted in any
form or by any means, electronic or
mechanical, including photocopy, recording
or any other information storage and retrieval
system, without prior permission in writing
from the publisher.

Printed and bound in Singapore by C.S. Graphics

Contents

The Three Great Lights in Masonry
are the Volume of Sacred Law, the
Square and the Compasses, and
the sacred writings are understood
to be those revered by the
individual Mason. Although there
are local variations in
Freemasonry's symbolic structure,
the Three Great Lights are
universal. Taken together they form
the most essential, as well as the
most widely known, of the Masonic
symbols. No Masonic Lodge can
meet unless they are present and
displayed. (Print, 1809)

The Pursuit of the Knowledge of One's Self

Throughout all times and in all cultures men and women have sought to acquire knowledge about human nature and the purpose of human existence. In their search they have made use of an enormous variety of disciplines which have promised to penetrate the mystery of human nature and give them greater insight into themselves. These traditions have generally recognized some purpose for humanity. They are almost always closely connected with the religion of the society in which they have developed and orientated toward its Deity. In the West they belong to a general body of thought called 'The Mysteries', which can be traced, in one form or another, more or less continuously through the history of Western civilization.

The Mysteries were a recognized public institution in the ancient world. Although they have been a major influence in western intellectual life as recently as the sixteenth and seventeenth centuries, they are difficult for us to understand today because they are based on a view of the world which is quite different from our contemporary scientific materialism. While our 'universe' is limited by the extent of physical phenomena, that of the ancient world was conceived as containing, in addition to all the material objects, vast non-material realms which were not available to ordinary perception but were still considered to be part of the universe as it was then understood. These were arenas for the exploits of the gods of ancient mythology. Events occurring within these non-material domains were considered to be governed by an extension of the same body of natural law which gave consistency to the world of ordinary experience; and those events were thought to have an important influence on the daily activity of human life. The Mysteries were schools which provided knowledge of those non-material realms and of the natural laws operating in them. Although their existence was widely recognized, they usually conducted their work in seclusion. Their knowledge was imparted by a process of development which was represented by advancement through a series of grades, and the instruction itself involved extensive ritual and an elaborate symbolic structure which was used to codify the principles as well as to communicate them. The objective was to train people to live in consonance with natural laws as they operate in the non-material domains. Although the laws were considered to be of Divine origin, the Mysteries were not usually religious. Generally speaking, they were more concerned with philosophy and morality than with theology and religion.

The content of the Mysteries, that is, the symbolic material which was used to convey their instruction, includes tales of men and women with remarkable powers. They encounter fantastic beasts while involved in astonishing adventures which are governed by arbitrary rules and occur in unlikely locations. All this sounds very abstract, more than a little superstitious, and quite irrelevant to our contemporary experience until we recognize that in our own terms the closest and most immediately available of these non-material domains is called the psyche. Each of us has similar adventures every time we dream, for the boundary of the inaccessible part of that domain is the threshold of one's own consciousness.

The symbols employed and the way in which they are used have made the Mysteries seem strange, even bizarre, to our twentieth-century perception, conditioned as it is by the materialistic orientation of our society. Nonetheless, in recent years and for a variety of reasons the

Mysteries and more particularly the areas with which they deal have become the subject of serious scholarly research. In the process it has become apparent that the Mysteries have seemed bizarre because we have tended to take them at face value; we have looked at symbols devised in another culture and in another time and interpreted them in the context of our contemporary, materialistic understanding, without sufficient regard for what they might have meant to those who formulated them. As a result we have dismissed them as superstition or, at best, as primitive groping toward our own science. Now it begins to appear that the Mystery traditions may, in fact, have something to say to us at a time when our paradigm of scientific materialism is proving to be incomplete.

But can we fit Freemasonry into this role? Is it plausible to suggest that a loosely associated group of large, contemporary organizations, occupying conspicuous premises, prominent in society, operating charities, hospitals and medical research facilities, claiming members from all races and social strata, and conducting their activities openly throughout the world is, in fact, a 'Mystery', an antique body of knowledge, traditionally carefully hidden, which provides instruction touching on the fundamental nature of humankind?

Although Masonry represents a single set of principles, it is not a single organization. There are a number of governing bodies called Grand Lodges which regulate the activities of Freemasonry within specific geographical areas. There is usually a Grand Lodge for each country (in the United States there is one for each State) in which there are Masonic activities. These Grand Lodges accord each other mutual recognition on the basis of certain well defined principles. In this way the Craft is able to reflect the character and temperament of a wide variety of cultural and social environments and at the same time preserve a consistent philosophical point of view. These principles, on which Grand Lodges throughout the world agree, can be summarized, in a general way, as follows.

Freemasonry is a very old, secular, fraternal society which requires the belief in a Supreme Being as its principal qualification for membership and which is dedicated to the practice of tolerance, respect and understanding of others; the encouragement of high standards of morality among its members; and the performance of charitable works. Freemasonry certainly is and does all these things; but in some hard-to-define way it seems to be 'something else' beyond those things. One looks for this additional dimension, in part, because Freemasonry has survived for almost three hundred years while other apparently similar fraternal organizations have disappeared; and, also, because throughout its history it has drawn members from the best minds and the most idealistic leaders of the day.

If a contemporary Mason were asked about that 'something else', he would probably say that it is an indescribable quality related in some way to the very rich and complex symbolic structure that is characteristic of the Craft. The Candidate for Masonry is introduced to that symbolic structure by participating in the ritual dramas, called 'Degrees', through which Freemasonry communicates its teaching of morality. The symbols are drawn, in part, from the practices of the medieval stone masons' guilds; and as part of the task of administering Masonic activities the Grand Lodges perform a role as the custodian of those symbols. In practice the Grand Lodges preserve this body of symbolism and protect it from change; but they do not interpret it. The Masonic Lectures, which purport to explain the material in the rituals, actually do no more than refer the reader to a large body of Renaissance literature and recommend that it be studied. The interpretation of the symbols, if it is to be done at all, is the responsibility of the individual Mason; and it is in the process of that personal interpretation – and of seeing the principles that emerge operate in one's own life – that one can see the Craft of Freemasonry come alive as a 'Mystery'.

The following pages look at one such individual interpretation. It is an unusual one, which will seem strange to many, perhaps to most, Masons; but it is an interpretation which is able to account for characteristics of the Order which seem puzzling in other contexts. It will suggest that the Renaissance scholars who were the originators of speculative Freemasonry considered their Craft to be a discipline which we today would identify with Psychology – or perhaps with the contemporary academic research into the nature of consciousness. It differs from contemporary psychology in that it is infused with the deep devotion to the Deity which characterized the Renaissance; and, of course, it states its psychological principles by employing the rich symbolic images which were characteristic of the sixteenth and seventeenth centuries. To understand such a perspective we have to look at the origins of the Craft, and to do that we must start much earlier than the Renaissance – with the Mason-Architects who built the cathedrals of the medieval period, and even before.

The Thread of the Mysteries

If we are to suggest that Freemasonry carries the teaching of the Mysteries in its symbolic structure, it is not unreasonable to ask questions such as, 'How did it come by that knowledge? Where did it discover this information which is notoriously hard to find?' Since the origins of Freemasonry itself are obscure, and apparently intentionally so, we should recognize at the outset that we are unlikely to uncover definitive answers to these significantly more difficult questions. However, there are two plausible answers; one is old and well known, and the other relatively new and not yet fully understood. The first, stated broadly, suggests that the mystical tradition has been found within the builder's craft since antiquity, that it blossomed in the climate of the Renaissance, and that it survived openly in England where it was relatively free from the influence and persecutions of the Reformation/ Counter-Reformation. This is not an entirely foolish idea.

The temples which we can still observe in the lands around the eastern Mediterranean provide evidence of the close association between architecture and mystical philosophy in the ancient world, particularly in Greece, where it was closely related to the pantheon. Today we are inclined to note that ancient Greece was a polytheistic society and, recognizing the merits of our monotheism, dismiss their many deities as mere mythology. In fact, the Greeks had made a religion of their psychology; properly understood, the personalities, crotchets, antics and exploits of their gods, as recorded in the Greek mythology, are a description of the Greeks' understanding of their own psychological processes. That is why the names of so many mythological characters have found their way so easily into contemporary psychological theory.

In the Greek culture much effort was made to capture the essence of these psychological phenomena in the stone structures related to each 'god'. Although most of the ancient Greeks probably took their religion at face value, where the introduction of an individual into the 'Mysteries' (into the understanding of his own psyche/spirit) was involved, the pantheon almost certainly formed part of the curriculum; and architectural forms seem to have played an important part in the instruction. The Roman architect, military engineer and philosopher, Vitruvius, who drew together the then existing architectural forms into what we know as the 'orders of architecture', provides an example of an architect much influenced by the Mysteries – in his case by the Dionysian tradition. In addition to his secular work he was deeply concerned with ways in which the essence of the pantheon and its underlying psychology could be translated into the experience of the physical world by the use of architectural techniques. He taught that buildings, particularly those with a religious function, should have dimensions which reflect the proportions of the human body. Appropriateness of style was another of his concerns; he indicated that temples dedicated to stern, warlike gods such as Minerva, Mars and Hercules, and buildings housing the activities they influenced, should be built using the austere Doric Order. Similarly, the Corinthian Order was said to be appropriate for buildings dedicated or relating to the delicate activities of such goddesses as Venus, Proserpine or the Nymphs, while the Ionic Order was considered suitable for buildings relating to deities such as Juno, Diana and Dionysus, who occupied the central ground of the pantheon.

There is no doubt that the sort of thinking exemplified by Vitruvius had a profound influence on the architectural practice of ancient Rome, as it did again in the Renaissance. However, it would be foolish to suggest that the operative stonecutters who built the cities of the Roman Empire were to a man serious students of the Ancient Mysteries. What is more likely is that a few of the more educated members of the Collegium Fabrorum (the Roman College which oversaw the activity of building) concerned themselves with philosophical considerations, which they understood in the context of their occupation, as well as with the practical business of construction; and it is among these that we may think that an architecturally orientated Ancient Mystery must have been practised and preserved.

How this body of esoteric knowledge was transmitted through medieval Christendom, and in particular to England where speculative masonry is acknowledged to have started, is a matter of conjecture. One might think that among the builders who accompanied the Roman army in the conquest of Britain there were some of the educated group who brought their mystical turn of mind with them (indeed, there is evidence of such a body of thought within the Roman army itself); and it is tempting to believe that these ancient craftsmen left some part of their organization behind when the Romans withdrew early in the fifth century. These, preserving their secret lore, would have kept themselves hidden until they could emerge about 900 CE to participate in the rise of the medieval guilds and infuse their tradition into the Freemasons Guild.

Unfortunately, that sort of line is difficult to trace in England. There is no direct evidence of it; in fact, the mason's trade virtually disappeared when almost all Roman buildings were destroyed by the Saxons who for two centuries built almost entirely of wood and thatch and in the next three hundred years did very little stone construction. It was not until around the year 1000 that serious building in stone began again in England; and even then English masons' guilds were slow to develop and were never really strong outside London. It is hard to imagine that a masonic or architecturally based mystical idiom could have survived intact under the circumstances which obtained in Saxon England.

In France, however, the situation was different. It seems probable that there was some direct development from the Roman colleges to the earliest continental medieval guilds; and whatever of the Ancient Mysteries were to be found in the Collegium Fabrorum could have been transmitted directly to the French masons' guild and from there to masons throughout the continent. Here we must avoid the temptation to believe the romantic tales of bands of mystical masons, members of a secret organization, who travelled across Latin Christendom building cathedrals. In reality cathedral building was only a part of medieval construction. Since the medieval nobility were in large measure concerned with fighting one another, castles and other fortifications occupied a large portion of their attention; and the surviving records indicate that masons were frequently conscripted to work on military (and later civic) projects. Unless masons working on a cathedral or abbey were specifically exempted – by no means always the case – they did not escape this sort of conscription; and we must assume that the overwhelming majority of masons did as much secular as religious building.

Nonetheless, the very scale of Europe's magnificent cathedrals testifies to the great importance that was attached to them and to the enormous attention that was given to their building, while the steady development of their architectural style and the progressive refinement of building techniques testify to the existence of specialists in the field. It is not unreasonable to think that a small core within the masons' guilds on the continent worked exclusively on sacred buildings, perpetuated a mystical tradition received from the Collegium, and passed it on to a few within their group who demonstrated an aptitude for that sort of interior work.

Nor is it difficult to imagine how such a teaching might be stated in Christian terms using symbols ready to hand on a cathedral building site. In the first place, a cathedral built in the Romanesque or Gothic style was, in itself, a means of instruction for a largely illiterate population; and it incorporated a representation of much of the traditional Western metaphysical system; thus:

the Nave represented the Earth, the habitation of the Church Militant, the residence of incarnate humanity. According to the medieval conception the Earth was the totality of physical existence. Today we would say that the Nave represents the physical universe;

the Choir represented Paradise and Purgatory, the habitation of the Church Penitent; it was the world of Angels, the residence of souls awaiting birth or, after death, awaiting judgment in the Planetary or Astral Spheres. We would call it the psyche;

the Sanctuary represented Heaven, the abode of the Church Triumphant; it was the world of Archangels, the Celestial Sphere in medieval cosmology. We would call it the Spirit;

Divinity Itself was present in the person of Christ through the Mystery of the Blessed Sacrament reserved in the Tabernacle on the altar. In some traditions the abode of Divinity is called the 'World Without End';

the Rood Screen separated the nave from the choir and permitted the ordinary worshipper only glimpses of the events taking place beyond in the same way

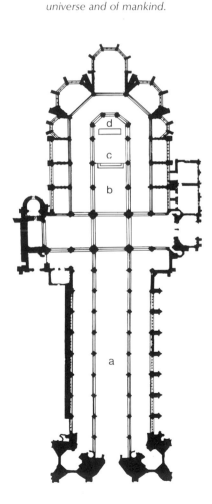

a Nave: *Physical World/Body*
b Choir: *Psyche/Soul*
c Sanctuary: *Spirit*
d Tabernacle: *Divinity*

that the threshold of consciousness separates ordinary awareness from Paradise and Heaven – which lie in, and beyond, what we call the unconscious;

three aisles, accessed by the three doors in the west wall, extended the length of the cathedral building and suggest an idea which finds its way into Freemasonry as the Rule of Three. This idea will be examined in some detail in due course.

It is significant that such an interpretation can be put on an unmodified cathedral plan, because any philosophical speculation into the nature of the psyche which was conducted outside the institutions of the Church would of necessity have been carried on with the utmost care. The period of cathedral building (mid-twelfth to end sixteenth century) was also the period during which the Church began to exhibit the materialism and internal strain which was to lead ultimately to the Reformation. Heresy was defined broadly, searched out vigorously, and suppressed ruthlessly; and, while the Mysteries need not conflict with the Church or its doctrines, the authorities of the day were not particularly discriminating in their investigations. In fact, the contradictory situation within the Church at that time presents a real puzzle. At the very time that the Church was constructing those enduring cathedrals whose exalted quality continues to enrich our lives today, it was entering a period during which it would perpetrate that most hideous of atrocities known as the Inquisition. It is difficult to understand this juxtaposition of barbarity and sacred building in a single society, and it is not unreasonable to suppose that the enduring spiritual quality of the cathedrals derives in part from a mystical orientation in the men who actually built them.

Tracing the thread of the Mysteries in this way does not require us to believe that Freemasonry, which is generally acknowledged to have started as an English institution, is of French or continental origin. Rather it suggests that a line of esoteric thought from the ancient world probably existed within the continental, particularly French, medieval masons' guilds. From there it could have been (re)introduced to the British Isles in a variety of ways. Norman masons were working in England as early as the tenth century and in vastly increased numbers after the time of the Norman Conquest in 1066. If these French masons had a mystical core teaching within their guilds, they would certainly have brought their traditions to Britain with their Norman Romanesque architectural style. According to this theory, the Mystery tradition would have been communicated from that source to those of the English cathedral building masons with a similar turn of mind.

There are other possibilities. For example, there was bitter conflict between England and Scotland around the turn of the fourteenth century, and from that time Scotland's cultural orientation shifted from England to the Continent. This change in perspective is observable in the Scottish architecture of the period – Melrose Abbey, for example, exhibits much French influence; and it is likely that the French masons involved would have come with their philosophical as well as their practical workings. These ideas would certainly have been reinforced when the Knights Templar were suppressed in 1313 and many of the surviving knights took refuge in Scotland where the Pope's directive dissolving the Order was never promulgated.

These speculations do not demonstrate that Freemasonry is a mystical tradition; rather they indicate that it is entirely plausible that a mystical tradition had been handed down through the medieval masons' guilds and that it most probably found its way to England where it would have been preserved by a small group within the trade. In time it would find a home within the principal organization of English builders, the London Company of Masons, where it could survive the persecutions of the Reformation/ Counter-Reformation and the rigours of the Thirty Years War.

The possibility of an esoteric core within the London Company of Masons is not a new idea. In Bernard Jones's *Mason's Guide and Compendium* (1950), we find, 'Straight from operative to speculative in English masonry might be to us a difficult journey, but from operative via a fraternity hidden away at the very heart of the craft and merging in the days of the Renaissance into an early form of modern symbolic masonry – yes, that is a sequence not only natural, but perfectly credible.' While the sort of process outlined above is natural and credible enough and no doubt close to the truth, as far as it goes; it is probably only part of the story. To see more of the picture we must look at the second possible answer to our original question about the source of Freemasonry's mystical connection. We find it in late-twentieth-century academic research into the history of Renaissance thought and in its understanding of the intellectual climate within which speculative Free-masonry came into being.

A New Look at the Renaissance

Until relatively recently the startling resurgence of art and intellectual activity which is called the Renaissance was thought to be the result of the interaction of two schools of thought, Scholasticism and Humanism. It is only since World War II that serious historians have recognized that the popular revival of Western mysticism in the late 1400s, in the form of what is now called the Hermetic/Kabbalistic tradition, was a third major influence. It is this third stream of thought that is of interest to us, both from the historical point of view and because some of today's Masonic material refers to the literature of this tradition. However, to understand the influence of this third school of thought properly we must first look briefly at the positions of the other two.

Scholasticism was the intellectual frame of reference of medieval Christianity, and by the time the Renaissance began it had been well established for a long time. When the Roman Empire finally collapsed in 410, Christianity had been its official religion for almost four generations. The Latin Church had adopted a Roman organizational structure and adminis-trative hierarchy which enabled it to fill the vacuum caused by the demise of the Empire; and in so doing the Church managed to preserve civilization in the West during the difficult period of the Dark Ages.

As a result of this role the Latin Church entered the medieval period as the predominant power in Western Christendom, and throughout that period the Church leadership acted to enhance and consolidate the secular as well as the spiritual dimension of its power. Like the society of the Middle Ages, the Church's intellectual posture was a static one; Christ had accomplished the one creative act required on earth by the establishment of His Church through the sacrifice of the Crucifixion and the miracle of the Resurrection; what remained was for Christians to produce on earth, under the direction of the Church, a replica of the Divine Kingdom in heaven. Progress, or development, or original thinking were not part of this intellectual paradigm; the human task was the endless celebration of the

Divine perfection manifested in the Christian miracle. The intellectual activity of the period, which was certainly monumental in its own way, was accomplished almost entirely within the confines of the Church, and consisted of the development of a doctrine which reconciled the Classical philosophers with the teachings of Christianity.

Humanism, which appeared first in Italy around the middle of the fourteenth century, represented a sharp contrast to Scholasticism. Its interest in the antique world was not as a support for Christianity, but for what the ancient philosophers had to say about mankind itself; and the humanist philosophers who emerged during the Renaissance saw man as 'the measure of all things'. This sort of thinking, which was bound to produce conflict in medieval society, developed in two directions. The first supported reform within the Church, and led finally to the Reformation; the second encouraged secular investigations and led eventually to modern critical and scientific thought.

The Western mystical tradition was introduced into this turbulent intellectual situation in the latter part of the fifteenth century. Two Florentines who were members of the Medici circle were particularly influential in this respect. Each drew his material from opposite ends of the Mediterranean. In about 1460 Cosimo di Medici purchased a manuscript which had been recovered from the library in Constantinople before it was captured by the Turks in 1453. The documents in the manuscript form a literature of mystical experience set out in an Egyptian/astrological idiom. They are known today as the *Hermetica*, and are recognized as having been written in the second or third century CE, probably in Alexandria. However, Marsilio Ficino, the Italian scholar and monk who translated them for Cosimo di Medici, conceived that they were the work of an Egyptian named Hermes Trismegistus whom he regarded as a contemporary of Moses. Because of this error, which was not discovered until the early seventeenth century, the Hermetica was regarded by Renaissance scholars as a pagan prophesy of Christianity, and it was thus (for a time, at least) an acceptable literature for study by Christian scholars.

Pico della Mirandola was a philosopher and writer and also a member of the Medici circle. His interests lay in the fragments of Kabbalah which found their way to Italy from the Jewish schools in Spain. There had been a rich exchange of ideas among the students of Christian, Muslim and Jewish mysticism during the period of Muslim rule, and with the expulsion of the Jews in 1492 a large volume of Kabbalistic literature was diffused throughout North Africa and Europe. A good deal of it found its way to Florence where Pico studied it enthusiastically. The Church allowed him to pursue his studies because in proving (at least to his own satisfaction) that Jesus was the Messiah by using Kabbalistic methods he was seen by the Church to provide Jewish authentication of Christianity.

Within the Roman Church itself there was a good deal of influential support for this body of Hermetic/Kabbalistic thought which was centred on the neo-platonic school at Florence. For example, Francisco Giorgi, a prominent Venetian, a noted politician and diplomat (Henry VIII consulted him in respect of his divorce from Catherine of Aragon), and a Franciscan monk, was the author of *Di Harmonia Mundi*, which treated the subject in detail. Near the end of the fifteenth century, when recognition of the need of some clerical reform was becoming widespread, he and others of his turn of mind proposed a combination of the Hermetic/Kabbalistic tradition and Franciscan mysticism as a means to infuse a new spirituality into the Church. In the event it was to be three-quarters of a century before the Church would be ready to undertake serious reform, and then it would be along the lines of restated conservatism rather than mystical revival. Nonetheless, with its foundation in the Medici circle and with substantial clerical support, the Hermetic/Kabbalistic tradition flourished in Italy during the early sixteenth century and spread through Germany, the Low Countries and England.

In 1542 the Church reconstituted the Papal Inquisition in response to the activities of the Protestant Churches in Italy; the Italian Renaissance and Italian mystical philosophy came to an end in the same year. The writings of men like Pico and Ficino were proscribed, and even the works of such a prominent churchman as Francisco Giorgi were censored. Further north, however, the influence of the Roman Church was not so strong, and the same forces which gave the Protestant Churches time and space to develop also created a situation in which such men as Erasmus, Agrippa, Dürer and Reuchlin could explore the Hermetic/Kabbalistic tradition without too much danger of persecution.

We know that the tradition was also studied in England during the second half of the sixteenth century, for when the Italian Hermeticist, Giordano Bruno, visited Oxford in 1583 he apparently attempted to pass off some of Ficino's writing as his own work and seems to have been treated in the unkindly fashion which Oxford dons still reserve for that sort of thing. There is, in fact, a great deal of evidence to indicate a lively interest in this Renaissance mystical tradition in England during the second half of the sixteenth century, the period in which speculative Masonry was almost certainly taking shape. The literary works of the period indicate that prominent writers such as Spenser, Sidney, Chapman, Shakespeare, Milton, Bacon and Fludd were all familiar with, and in some cases active advocates and practitioners of, the Hermetic/Kabbalistic tradition. That influential – and misrepresented – figure, John Dee, is known to have had all the major works on the subject in his library; and his Introduction to the English translation of *Euclid* indicates his familiarity with the material.

These scholars, in common with many in the Renaissance academic community, had a particular view of the world which is not commonly found among academics, or among Westerners in general, today. They seem to have regarded the Physical World, the Psyche, the Spirit, and Divinity as a spectrum of phenomena, a sort of dimension. Along this dimension one could, with appropriate training, be conscious at various levels. The mastery of this 'Dimension of Consciousness', which spans the whole of existence from the material to the Divine, and the ability to operate at the several levels along it, was the objective which appears to have been pursued by a large part of the Renaissance academic community in the sixteenth and seventeenth centuries.

Here, at the start of the seventeenth century, our focus must narrow to England for it is there that we will find the threads which most probably lead to the formation of the first Masonic Lodges; most certainly it is there that the first public appearance of speculative Masonry is to be observed. When James I and VI came to the throne in 1603 the stimulating intellectual situation which had characterized Elizabethan England changed significantly. James was a superstitious man, markedly fearful of the Renaissance mystical traditions, probably because he confused them with witchcraft. He turned his back on all aspects of this very significant area of Renaissance thought; and it seems certain that those who wished to pursue an interest in the Hermetic/Kabbalistic tradition after his succession had to exercise the utmost discretion. This situation continued throughout the whole of the turbulent seventeenth century and the activities of such people are much harder to trace after 1603. In the 1650s there is evidence of involvement with the Renaissance mystical traditions among the members of the 'Invisible College', the probable ancestor of the Royal Society, which met first in London and then in Oxford. We find that they, too, felt the need to distance themselves, at least publicly, from those traditions before the Society was actually founded.

In the first quarter of the seventeenth century, at about the same time that discreet conduct with respect to the practice of the Mysteries became necessary, we find records in the Worshipful Company of Freemasons of the City of London of members 'coming on the Accepcon', a phrase which is generally taken to indicate the existence of a philosophical or speculative fraternity of 'accepted masons' within that organization of operative craftsmen. By the mid-1600s the Masons Company was in serious decline as a body controlling the building trade in London. Masonic historians consider it to be a strong presumption that by 1665 a substantial, and growing, proportion of the membership of the London Company of Masons were speculative Masons – Masons who had been accepted into the interior philosophical fraternity without being associated with the operative craft.

So here is the situation in seventeenth-century England. On the one hand, at the start of the century there is a prominent body of influential and educated men who are known to be interested in the Hermetic/Kabbalistic tradition; and during the turbulent middle decades of the century these have found it necessary to be progressively more guarded in the pursuit of their interests. On the other hand, there is an operative Builders Guild in decline, which by 1665 is known to have an increasing membership of gentlemen whose interests are in the mystical teaching believed to be preserved at the core of the guild. About fifty years later, in 1717, four Lodges which have been meeting 'from time immemorial' band together publicly to form the Grand Lodge, the first recognized speculative Masonic organization; and they have a system of symbolism which borrows heavily from the material of both the Operative Mason's Craft and the Western Mystical tradition. It does not require much of a leap of imagination to draw these two lines together and to suggest that among the 'Accepted Masons' within the London Company were in fact some of those educated men who, in fear of their lives, pursued their mystical interests in discrete privacy; and, indeed, there is abundant evidence in the periodicals of the time to show that the existence of such a group was generally acknowledged.

The philosophical studies of the Craft must have been very much in touch with the thinking of the time because from its small beginnings in London in 1717 Freemasonry spread very quickly. For example, Grand Lodges were established in Ireland in 1725, in Scotland in 1736, in Germany in 1737, in Denmark in 1745, and in the Netherlands in 1756. The date of the first French Masonry is obscure, but it is certainly prior to 1735. Lodges under the English Constitution were set up in the American Colonies very early; in

Boston in 1733, in Charleston in 1735, and also in Savannah, Philadelphia and New York at about the same time. The Craft was to prove very popular with the Colonial intellectual community, and it was to have a profound influence on the founding of the United States. During the Napoleonic era French Masons established Lodges throughout the Mediterranean basin and in much of Africa, and in the nineteenth century Lodges under the Dutch and English Constitutions were established throughout the entire world.

Freemasonry as Psychology

To understand this transcultural organization as a 'Mystery', we will find a place for Freemasonry in the framework of Renaissance thought outlined above by deriving a psychology from the Craft's symbolic structure. Since Masonry in each country has its own characteristics which reflect the national temperament, a complete treatment of the subject would be a vastly complex undertaking. In order to make the task manageable in the space of these pages it will be necessary to focus our attention on a particular form of Masonic symbolism; and we will use the one employed by the United Grand Lodge of England. It is a form which is readily accessible, in wide use through the world; and it is also fairly typical of the ritual as it is conducted elsewhere, particularly by the Craft in America. Since the general Masonic principles are universally preserved by all Grand Lodges, readers who are familiar with forms of Masonic symbolism which are used on the Continent of Europe and in other parts of the world should be able to relate our findings to their own experience without difficulty. Our 'Masonic Psychology' will be a developmental psychology because growth was implicit in the organismic paradigm of the Renaissance, and it will be orientated toward the Deity. In this respect, although we will use much contemporary terminology, our ideas will contrast with the psychology of today which is, with some notable exceptions, based on the materialistic assumptions of twentieth-century science.

We will start by defining the framework within which Freemasonry operates, a very different framework from the materialism which characterizes our industrial society. Indeed, Freemasonry presupposes the metaphysical system we saw embodied in the plan of the Gothic cathedral. It describes that metaphysics by considering the 'regular progression of science from a point to a line, from a line to a superficies, from a superficies to a solid'. This idea, which is quoted from the ritual of the Second Degree, is actually a neo-platonic device using a mathematical idiom to describe the process by which the Deity brings the Universe into existence. From this geometrical perspective the process starts with a point as the fundamental element; the point moves, and in doing so generates a line; the line moves, in a direction not parallel to itself, and generates a plane (superficies); the plane, moving in a similar way, generates a solid.

The geometrical characteristics of this succession of figures are such that each action brings a new object into being which has its own characteristics, but which also contains — and includes the characteristics of — the object which generated it. Thus, for example, the solid, which is defined by the rules of three-dimensional geometry, contains the plane from which it was generated; and the laws of solid geometry are those of plane geometry with some additional complexity. The neo-platonists used this geometrical idiom to describe the process by which Divinity (the Point, the fundamental, essential, Source-Of-All) projected Itself into existence, through the

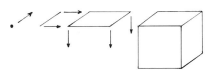

The 'regular progression of science from a point to a line, from a line to a superficies, from a superficies to a solid' is the way in which Freemasonry explains the process by which the Deity brings the four levels of existence into being. It is a neo-platonic device which can be traced through the literature of the Renaissance, via medieval Spain, to Alexandria.

progressively more complex levels of the Spirit (line); the Psyche (superficies) and finally Materiality (solid); each of these 'worlds' containing within itself the next higher level from which it was derived. The same story is to be found in a mystical interpretation of Genesis when God 'creates' the World of the Spirit (Chap. I); 'forms' the World of the Psyche (Chap. II), and finally expels (projects) Adam and Eve into the Physical World by the process of incarnation. We can see, of course, that this is the same metaphysical scheme that we found to be implicit in the Cathedral plan and also the same hierarchy we observed along the 'dimension of consciousness' which was envisioned by the Renaissance scholars. It is, indeed, the basis of almost all Western philosophy prior to the nineteenth century. In the context of this scheme the physical sciences, which began to emerge during the latter part of the Renaissance, are concerned with the Solid, with the physical world; and today their practitioners generally ignore, or deny the existence of, all the other levels of the progression.

Freemasonry is concerned with the superficies, that is, with the psyche; but, unlike contemporary science, it does not ignore the other parts of the metaphysical system. On the contrary, Freemasonry is based on the premise that the individual who explores his psyche can, and should, be committed to and guided by his God as well as continuing his active role in the physical world. It is for this reason that belief in a Supreme Being is a prerequisite for membership in the Order and that its members are admonished to pursue their respective religions with diligence. Beyond that fundamental requirement, the nature of a Mason's God, the Scripture he uses, and the form of his worship are not of concern to the Craft.

Freemasonry conceives of the complete human being as having a body, a psyche/soul, a spirit and a contact with his Divine Source. It supposes that the human psyche also contains four levels which reflect that larger four-level structure. In specific terms it represents the psyche by the Temple of Solomon which it describes as a three-storey temple within which one can be conscious of the presence of Divinity. We will draw a parallel between these three storeys – the Ground Floor, the Middle Chamber, and the Holy of Holies – and the three levels of awareness in Jung's psychological model – the individual consciousness, the personal unconscious, and the collective unconscious. We should not be surprised to find these and other parallels between the two systems. They are, after all, studies of the same thing – simply conducted in two different periods in our culture, three hundred years apart.

The Masonic Candidate is introduced to this three-storey temple by participating in the Ceremonies of Three Degrees by which he advances in titular rank from his start as an Entered Apprentice, through the intermediate Degree of Fellowcraft, to the final Degree of Master Mason. This process usually takes place over a period of a few months. If he wishes to practice the Craft as a Mystery, as a means of psychological development, the new Master Mason will thereafter spend many years considering the implications of the Craft's symbolism and observing its principles operating in his life. If he perseveres, he will recapitulate – in the events of his day-to-day experience – the ritual progress he made through the symbolic degrees; and by this means he will, in time, achieve the sort of psychological maturity which his title of Master Mason implies. It is a long and arduous undertaking; indeed, it is the labour of a lifetime.

When the Candidate is admitted into Freemasonry the Ceremony of Initiation is conducted in an Entered Apprentice's Lodge which is held, figuratively, on the Ground Floor of King Solomon's Temple. The Ground Floor represents that part of the psyche which is in intimate contact with the material world. It is, to use Jungian terms, the individual consciousness. Although the First Degree and its work relates entirely to the Ground Floor, the Candidate is introduced to the idea that there are upper floors in the temple which he will explore as he advances in the Craft. These upper floors, which are said to be restricted to Brethren of higher Masonic rank, represent the candidate's unconscious, and this symbol gives us an explanation of the much misunderstood subject of Masonic secrecy. The Craft represents the unconscious by a body of material which is said to be 'secret'. As the Candidate advances in Masonic rank – symbolizing progressive psychological development – these 'secrets' are revealed in the successive Degrees which represent the insights into the unconscious which are characteristic of the maturing individual.

When the Candidate is advanced to the Second Degree the Ceremony of Passing is conducted in the Fellowcraft's Lodge which is held, figuratively, in the Middle Chamber of King Solomon's Temple. The Middle Chamber of the allegorical temple represents the soul, which has many characteristics of the personal unconscious (again using Jung's terminology); and when we look at the symbolism of a Fellowcraft's Lodge we will see that labour in the Second Degree involves serious psychological work. Continuing for the moment with Jungian terminology, the Master Mason's Lodge represents a level which corresponds in a general way to the collective unconscious. Such a Lodge is said to meet 'in the porchway entrance to the Holy of Holies', which we may understand to be that part of the psyche which is in intimate contact with the Spirit in a way similar to the manner in which the Ground Floor is in contact with the body. Lastly, working within this psychological structure, particularly at the higher levels, one can be conscious of the presence of Divinity.

Within a Masonic Lodge, which is a physical representation of the allegorical structure described above, there is always to be found a composite symbol called the Three Great Lights, composed of the Volume of the Sacred Law, the Square and the Compasses. Some of these objects have more than one meaning in Craft symbolism, but in this most fundamental symbol they represent the three upper levels of the individual's metaphysical structure. The Square represents the Psyche, the Compasses represent the Spirit, and the Sacred Writings represent Divinity, the Divine source from which they are received. The various configurations in which these objects are presented in each Degree describe the extent to which the psyche of the individual is under the influence of his spirit, while all the configurations emphasize the fact that the individual, as well as the entire universe, has its source and foundation in the Deity which sustains the whole structure.

Although the newly made Mason is restricted in his activities to the Ground Floor – his individual consciousness of the physical world – he is introduced to a number of principles by which, according to the Mysteries, the universe (and his own psyche) operates; and in considering these principles we can get some clue about the dynamics of the psyche as it is represented by the Craft. The Tracing Board of the First Degree is a drawing

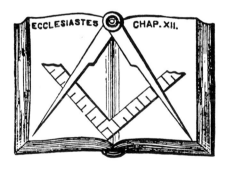

The Three Great Lights

The Furniture of the Lodge is said to consist of the Volume of Sacred Law, the Square and the Compasses. Taken together they are known as the Three Great Lights and no Lodge can work without their being displayed. In Christian countries the Volume of Sacred Law is usually taken to be the Bible, but as one travels East it is not uncommon to find Lodges displaying the Koran, the Torah, the Vedas, the Zend-Avesta, or some other scripture which reflects the religious persuasion of the Brethren composing the Lodge.

First Degree Tracing Board

Tracing Boards are visual aids used to illustrate the principles taught in each Degree. This First Degree Tracing Board represents, in highly formalized symbolism, the individual human being and his place in the Four Worlds.

which appears, at first, to be a heterogeneous collection of Masonic symbols but is actually an integrated picture used to illustrate the operation of these universal principles. We will look at the major ones.

The Ornaments of the Lodge are the Chequered Pavement, the Indented or Tessellated Border and the Blazing Star which is sometimes depicted as a Glory; taken together these describe what we may call the Law of Unity. The Blazing Star or Glory represents the entire relative universe as it is in reality – from the point of view of the Deity; a single, consistent, glorious manifestation of the Deity itself. The Chequered Pavement represents the universe as it appears to us who are incarnate in the physical world; alternate black and white, active and passive, easy and difficult – at best complementary, often seeming to be in opposition. But the characteristic of a squared pavement is that the individual pieces fit together to form a single integrated whole, the pavement itself. This notion is emphasized by the Border which binds the thing together as a single entity, a single, interactive system in which each element relates to and affects each of the others.

The Law of Duality is represented on the First Degree Tracing Board at several different levels. At the most general level (of the Spirit) it is shown as the Sun and the Moon and Stars. The fierce, brilliant, constant Sun and the gentle, pale, changeable Moon are ancient symbols for complementarity, and are perhaps the most fundamental symbolic representations of that principle which is echoed at the most detailed and materialistic level by the black and white squares of the pavement. At the intermediate level of the psyche the idea of duality is represented by the Doric and Corinthian columns; these are part of a more complex idea which we will consider shortly. The Law of Duality is also represented in terms of the individual human being by the two parallel lines which bound the 'point-within-a-circle'. In the English workings these refer to Moses (the Prophet) and Solomon (the Lawgiver), roles which convey the idea of exuberance and restraint. The notion of complementarity is even more obvious in the American usage where the parallel lines are associated with St John the Baptist (mid-summer) and St John the Evangelist (mid-winter). The Principle of Duality states that whenever anything is perceived in such a way that it appears to exist separate from its Divine Source, its complement also appears to exist to provide a balance for it. The placement of symbols of duality at various levels on the board is a reminder that the phenomenon of duality and the potential for polarization and opposition occur as soon as there is any sense of separation from the wholeness of Divinity; thus it is a principle which relates to the entire psychological world.

The principle referred to in the old Masonic texts as the 'Rule of Three' is represented most obviously on the First Degree Tracing Board by the three columns which are among its most prominent features. Their different architectural styles convey the idea (using a device borrowed from Vitruvius) that there are three 'agencies' which extend through all the levels of the Lodge/psyche: an active, exuberant, creative, expansive agency (the Corinthian Column); a passive, reflective, traditional, containing agency (the Doric Column); and a balanced, conscious, coordinating agency which has the task of keeping the other two in dynamic equilibrium (the Ionic Column). This concept will feature prominently in the discussion of Masonic labour.

The Lodge, as we have seen, has four levels, and these are reflected on the Tracing Board. The Chequered Pavement represents the Ground Floor, in intimate contact with the physical world. The middle area – dominated by the columns — represents the Middle Chamber of the soul, the essence of the Psyche; and the Heavens refer to the Porchway Entrance, in intimate contact with the Spirit. The Fourth Level, Divinity Itself, is represented by the Glory in the centre of the Board.

The Cardinal Points of the Compass on the Border of the Tracing Board define the East–West direction which has considerable importance in the Craft's symbolism as we shall see. It is the direction of the 'Dimension of Consciousness' which was mentioned earlier as the concern of the student of Renaissance mysticism.

On the First Degree Tracing Board Jacob's Ladder is depicted as offering a pathway in the East–West direction. This symbol, which represents hierarchical levels of consciousness, has various forms. For the moment it is enough to note that the Ladder has three principal rungs: Faith, Hope and Charity. These represent the appropriate frames of mind for individuals in each of the Three Degrees; Faith for the Apprentice, who is ignorant of the nature of the thing to which he aspires, and must trust in those who teach him; Hope for the Fellowcraft, who can glimpse enough of the nature of the goal to cause him to yearn for it; and Charity for the Master Mason who has achieved his goal and is able to nurture those junior to him.

The symbolic structure which we have discussed thus far forms the general introduction to metaphysics given to the Entered Apprentice, the new student of the Mysteries, at the start of his Masonic career. It is a representation of the psychological world as a whole and a general description of the field of Masonic labour. Before considering the nature of the labour to be accomplished in terms of psychological development in each Degree there is one more group of symbols, already referred to peripherally, which requires attention. These are the Point-within-the-circle-bounded-by-two-parallel-lines, the Volume of Sacred Law, and the representation of Jacob's Ladder.

These objects frequently appear together, even on older Tracing Boards; and should be interpreted as a single symbol. Together they represent an individual human being within the psychological world. The two parallel lines symbolizing the active and passive principles represent in the individual those same exuberant and constraining qualities that are illustrated by the Corinthian and Doric Columns for the psychological world at large. The balancing function is the 'column of consciousness', represented in the psychological world by the Ionic Column, and in the psyche of the individual human being by the Ladder with its three principal rungs: Faith, Hope and Charity. These three divisions suggest that the individual psyche has three major levels (corresponding to the three degrees). The Circle, which is bounded by the parallel lines, and the Volume of Sacred Law represent the radius of consciousness of the individual when he starts his work, and it indicates that at this stage of development one is able to perceive only the symbol of the Deity (the Volume of Sacred Law). The Ladder extending from the Chequered Pavement in the West to the Glory in the East suggests that by extending one's awareness, one has the capacity to be conscious of the presence of the Deity Itself.

The principles outlined above define the Masonic model of the psyche. The Mason who follows the Craft as a way of personal growth comes to know these ideas first as intellectual concepts and then, with practice, he becomes aware of their reality through his experience in the course of his day-to-day activity in the physical world. This is, in fact, a very old approach to individual development. It is based on the idea that if one makes a real effort to understand one's self, one's motivations and one's behaviour, the Deity (or Its agents) will provide the experiences which will facilitate that learning. During the Ceremony of Initiation the Candidate is told, '. . . without neglecting the ordinary duties of your station in life, you are expected to make a daily advance in Masonic knowledge'; a plain instruction to the Candidate that he is expected to observe what is happening in his life, interpret it in the context of the Craft's symbolism, and learn from the experience. Symbolically, he is introduced to the sort of events he can expect by the device of the ritual dramas called the Three Degrees.

The First Degree – Entered Apprentice

When the Candidate is first admitted into a Masonic Lodge his condition as an Entered Apprentice is represented by the Rough Ashlar, the first of a set of three symbols which the Craft calls the Three Immovable Jewels. An ashlar is a building stone; a rough ashlar is a stone which has not yet been shaped into the form required by its place in the structure. Freemasonry regards humanity as a 'Temple of God'; and the obvious implication – that the Candidate is expected to use the experiences of his own life to work on himself and to make himself into a stone properly 'shaped' to take his own unique place in that Temple – is exactly the one that is intended. However, there is more to the symbol than simply that. The rough ashlar is an individual stone, a stone which has been cut from the bedrock. In human terms it represents an individual human being. Now, a person can, if he chooses, regard himself as being essentially a member of a group or society with no personal control over his circumstance; he flows with that group or society, depends upon it for his support, takes its values as his own: and the experiences of his life are those of the members of the society. Such a person is, like the building stone which has not yet been cut from the bedrock, a part of the general mass.

In participating in the ceremony of the First Degree the Candidate receives, symbolically, a look into the nature of his own psyche. If he gives serious attention to the work of his Lodge and tries to understand it in the way we have outlined, there will come (sooner or later) a moment when 'it all comes together' and he sees his interior being as it is represented by the symbolism. When he has had such a look in fact, when he has had a real (not symbolic) experience which indicates that he is an individual, which proves to him that the thoughts he thinks and the decisions he takes have a real, tangible, usually immediate, effect on his life and on the lives of others; when he has once had even a glimpse into the workings of his psyche, he can never forget it. He cannot 'unsee' what he has seen; he can never put aside what that glimpse of his interior has taught him. A person with this sort of insight can, and should, remain committed to the well-being of others and to the advancement of his society in general. But, just as the Rough Ashlar which has been cut from the quarry will thereafter be an individual stone, such a person will be an individual, with individual responsibility for his actions and for the situations in which he finds himself for as long as he lives. The material which makes up the First Degree encourages the Candidate to take such a deep look at himself and at the workings of his psyche, and it is for this reason that one must ask to become a Mason. No one should be persuaded to assume that sort of responsibility until he feels he is ready for it.

Individual responsibility for one's actions is a concept which will be developed as the Candidate progresses through the degrees, and here, at the start of his Masonic career, the Candidate receives a clue as to how that development will take place. Within the Lodge there are seven Officers; when the Lodge is considered as a model of the psyche these seven Officers identify seven levels of consciousness. This idea is developed more fully in the Second Degree, but in the Opening in the First Degree we are told that the Inner Guard must be 'under the command of the Junior Warden'. The Inner Guard, as we will see presently, represents the level of consciousness which today is called the 'ego'; and the ritual tells the Apprentice to place his ego under the control of some agency within his psyche called the Junior Warden, which is similar to the 'Self' in Jungian terminology. In other words, the establishment of this 'command relationship' refers to a process similar to the emergence of the archetype of the Self. In examining this notion we can get an idea of the nature of Masonic labour.

To many people the ego consciousness seems to be themselves, and before they can place it under the control of the Self they must first recognize that the ego is not 'them', but a level of consciousness which is theirs to use. Now the ego has access to a number of modes of operation; and the Masonic system recognizes three: acting, thinking and feeling, which it represents by its rituals, its lectures and its devotions. By participating in these activities while observing his mental processes at the same time, the individual is able to see his ego operate, and to identify it as something which belongs to him. In addition, he can observe the personae, the various images which the Inner Guard/ego establishes to relate the individual to the world in the various social situations of his life. Most important, by habitually 'turning inside' for an insight into his internal state, he becomes aware of the existence of the Junior Warden/Self and of the fact that, if he listens, he has access to excellent internal guidance. At first this guidance comes as a feeling or 'hunch'; with practice it can be refined into a very reliable faculty. This 'command relationship' between the Inner Guard and the Junior Warden is called the 'Path of Honesty' in some traditions, because its establishment requires not only that the Candidate 'asks inside', but also that he be scrupulously honest with himself. Such honesty causes him to examine his conscience, and to begin questioning the habitual behaviour of a lifetime. To set up this 'command relationship' between the Inner Guard and the Junior Warden, to initiate the emergence of the Self and to turn to it for guidance, is one of the most important of the labours of the Entered Apprentice.

His other principal task is to bring into balance the part of the psyche which is in contact with the physical world. We have seen in our consideration of the three columns on the Tracing Board that there are three principles which operate throughout all the levels of the psyche in the form of active and passive functions held in balance by acts of consciousness. In each of the Degrees these functions are represented by Working Tools appropriate for labour at that level, and on the Ground Floor these Working Tools are tools of action. They describe those psychological functions closely related to the physical world. The tools of an Apprentice are: the Common Gavel, an active tool of force which we equate with the

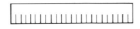

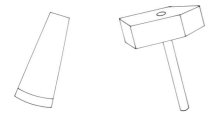

First Degree Working Tools

Tools are the physical objects which are employed by a craftsman to accomplish his work, and their use generally implies an acquired skill. Masonically, the Working Tools represent psychological capacities which the Mason must identify, gain control of, and then use in his daily life. In the First Degree the Gavel of passion, the Chisel of analysis and the 24″ Gauge of measured choice are tools of action suited for work in the physical world.

psychological capacity to experience passion, and which we should interpret to include joy, rage, intense commitment, etc.; the Chisel, a passive, containing tool – it receives the blows of the Gavel and directs them in a very precise way – which we can equate with the capacity for analysis, classification, calculation and rational thought; and the Twenty-four-inch Gauge, a tool of measurement by which the other two functions are directed and held in balance. The twenty-four inches have an obvious reference to time, and we may refine that idea by calling to mind the Biblical passage '. . . for everything there is a season . . .'. The Twenty-four-inch-Gauge represents the conscious capacity to identify the psychological function which is appropriate for the moment.

Equipped with this concept, the individual undertakes first to become aware of the three 'tools' (actually, the capacities they represent) in his psychological make-up, then to bring them under conscious control and finally to keep them in balance. He does this 'without neglecting the ordinary duties of [his] station in life', that is, by applying the concepts to the day-to-day events of his own life. As anyone who has tried to come to terms with a violent temper or a long-standing obsession with detail will recognize, the business of bringing the Working Tools of analysis and passion under conscious control involves substantial hard work, and this gives a certain realism to the term 'Masonic labour'. If he perseveres, however, the person who works in this way begins to recognize that he *reacts* to events less and less frequently and instead finds himself selecting his actions from an increasingly comprehensive repertoire of responses.

This greater choice is the start of what the individual can properly call 'my will'; and with that capacity for greater choice comes the opportunity to make selfish, malicious and destructive choices and the responsibility to choose courses of action which are constructive and integrating. There is a part of the ceremony of both the First and Second Degrees in which the Candidate is required to demonstrate a small bit of the ritual to the Wardens. This 'testing by the Wardens' represents the interior processes of conscience by which the developing individual is guided and encouraged to place voluntary limitation on his emerging capacity to choose. This process of self-discipline generally requires that he consider his motivations; and since these are frequently unconscious, the effort leads quite naturally to the Second Degree.

The Second Degree – Fellowcraft

Since the symbolism of the Craft comprises a developmental psychology, it envisages that the step to the Second Degree proceeds naturally as a result of progress in the First. This natural maturation which relates to the gradual emergence of the Self is indicated in Masonic symbolism by likening the newly made Fellowcraft to a ripened Ear of Corn. The Apprentice who is in control of the lower part of his psyche and whose Junior Warden/Self has become active has matured to a state in which he is ready to examine the more interior aspects of his psychological processes. Work at this level occurs in a part of the psyche which the Craft refers to as the Middle Chamber; it is in many ways similar to what Jung called the personal unconscious and to what is traditionally known as the soul.

The general approach to the work of the Fellowcraft is set out on the Second Degree Tracing Board which is an interior view and gives the

Second Degree Tracing Board

The Tracing Board of the Second Degree is a detailed drawing of the human individual who was shown in his environment on the First Degree Board. Here Jacob's Ladder is shown as a symbolic interior staircase which the individual must climb as he turns his attention away from the physical world to examine the nature of his soul and the workings of his own psychological processes.

impression of entering more deeply into the Temple. The Second Degree Board is a detailed drawing of a part of the First; specifically, of the Point-within-a-circle-bounded-by-two-parallel-lines and the Jacob's Ladder. The two parallel lines are shown in the Second Degree as the two pillars (here identified as complementary or opposite by association with the Pillars of Cloud and Fire from Exodus and by the terrestrial and celestial spheres surmounting them), while the Ladder is replaced on the Second Degree Tracing Board by the Winding Staircase. Like the Ladder on the First Degree Board, the Staircase extends in the East–West direction and defines the 'dimension of consciousness' from materiality to Divinity. The person who wishes to practice the Craft as a Mystery is expected to ascend through these various levels of consciousness which the symbol describes. On the First Degree Tracing Board we saw the Ladder divided into 'three principal rounds', corresponding to the Three Degrees of the Craft and describing three principal levels of psychological consciousness relating to body, soul and spirit. The Winding Staircase serves a similar function but communicates more complex ideas and presents them in greater detail.

The Staircase is among the most complicated of the Craft's symbols and a consideration of all its implications is beyond our scope. In the most general terms the Winding Staircase defines seven 'levels of consciousness', from consciousness of the physical body at the bottom to consciousness of the Spirit and Divinity at the top. By summarizing a large body of ritual and lecture, we can say that the Stairs assign a step or level of consciousness to each of the seven Officers of the Lodge; and with each of these it associates a great deal of Classical literature relating to the Seven Liberal Arts and Sciences and the Classical Schools of Architecture. It also associates the three Principal Officers of the Lodge with the Three Grand Masters who presided at the building of King Solomon's Temple – Solomon, King of Israel, who conceived the project; Hiram, King of Tyre, who provided the materials; and Hiram Abiff, the Principal Architect. This connection will be of real significance when we consider the Masonic Legend in the Third Degree. In this way the seven Officers of the Lodge are seen to represent seven levels or stages on the East–West 'dimension of consciousness', while the staircase symbolism points to a body of literature which provides information and instruction about each level.

Strictly speaking, a state of consciousness cannot be described – it must be experienced; but we can catch a very incomplete glimpse of the idea the Craft tries to communicate about each of these levels of consciousness by considering each Officer of the Lodge in the context of one of the Seven Liberal Arts and Sciences.

Tyler or Outer Guard is associated with Grammar, the Art which sets out strict rules for structuring ideas in order that they can be communicated and recorded in the physical world. The Tyler represents that part of the psyche which is in intimate contact with the physical body through the central nervous system. It is a 'guard' in that it protects the psyche from being overwhelmed by stimuli from the physical world.

Inner Guard is associated with Logic, the Art which teaches rules for rational analysis; highly structured, but entirely psychological. It represents what contemporary psychology refers to as the ego, the habit-following executive of day-to-day psychological activity which is distinguished by its capacity to form

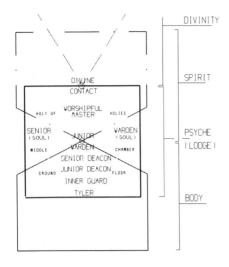

Four Worlds with Officers

In one sense the Psyche (represented by the Lodge) forms a bridge in consciousness between the physical and spiritual worlds. The Seven Officers of the Lodge represent seven levels of consciousness which make this connection.

mental images. It is a 'guard' in the sense that it provides the personae that enable the psyche to relate to the world.

Junior Deacon is associated with Rhetoric, the Art which teaches persuasive and impressive writing by invoking the feelings of the reader. The Junior Deacon represents the psychological level of feelings and moods, a careful examination of which gives a clue to events which are occurring in the unconscious. In the Classical world Rhetoric also contains instruction in the art of memory; and the Junior Deacon, representing a level of awareness near the threshold of ordinary consciousness, relates to the capacity to recall events from memory.

Senior Deacon is associated with the Science of Arithmetic, a subject used for training in the manipulation and representation of abstract ideas. The Senior Deacon represents the level of Awakening. To be 'awake' in this sense is to be present in the moment, to be aware of events as they occur both in the world and within one's own psyche, to understand their implication, and to see the threats and opportunities they imply.

Junior Warden is associated with the Science of Geometry, as the Second Lecture puts it, 'a Science whereby we find out the contents of bodies unmeasured by comparing them with those already measured'. The Junior Warden is similar to the Self, as the term is used by Jungian psychologists. The somewhat obtuse Masonic definition of geometry quoted above begins to take on greater meaning when one recognizes that it alludes to the old principle of 'as above, so below'. In the process of Masonic labour the Self is expected to emerge into consciousness and then to find out the contents of the unconscious by the observation of day-to-day experience.

Senior Warden is associated with the Science of Music, which had a much broader and more mystical connotation to the Renaissance scholar than it does to us today. As a Science, Music is based largely on the ratios between the frequencies of each note, on the manner in which time is structured, and upon the way these are combined to produce specific effects. The Senior Warden can be seen to represent the level of the soul; and the association with Music suggests the soul's task of maintaining a harmonious relationship among all the components of the psyche.

Worshipful Master is associated with the Science of Astronomy (which certainly meant Astrology to the framers of the symbolic structure). As the observation of the heavens was thought to reveal the intentions of the Deity, Astronomy suggests a level of consciousness which can see at a broad, transpersonal scale, and can perceive the intent of the Divine Plan. The level of consciousness represented by the Worshipful Master is in intimate contact with the Spirit in a manner analogous to the Tyler's relationship to the physical body.

In this way the Second Degree Tracing Board and its associated ritual define (in symbolic terms) seven 'levels of consciousness' within the psyche which, when developed and brought to mature functioning, comprise a conscious connection between Divinity and the physical world.

The Winding Staircase is flanked by two columns. We have already noted that these two columns are complementary – active and passive; and the fact that they are introduced in the Second Degree relates them in some way to the personal unconscious. They are said to be made of brass, cast in the clay ground – characteristics which relate them to the physical world, and to be hollow to contain the archives of the Craft. Taken together these ideas, an archival record, stored in the personal unconscious, and relating to events in the physical world, suggest that the columns are a representation of an individual's memory organized in such a way that memories which constrain and inhibit are found in one place while those which enliven and move to action are found in another. By introducing this idea in the Second Degree, in connection with the Middle Chamber of the soul, the symbolism indicates that the memories referred to are of a particular sort, quite deep in the unconscious, not ordinarily accessible but available when one works at that level of consciousness. We are, of course, drawing a parallel with the super ego/ego ideal as described by Freud or with the emotional and intellectual complexes identified by Jung – in this case classified into active and constraining groups.

The memories such as those stored in the two columns in the Second Degree are known to have a profound, though unconscious, effect on individuals and society alike. At the individual level they compel and circumscribe a person's behaviour, while at the social level they define the society's concepts of morality. Circumscribed behaviour of this sort is useful (even essential) to enable an individual to fit into a family and its immediate social circle, particularly during childhood; but adult behaviour which is thus circumscribed is often unrewarding, frequently unproductive, and sometimes actually harmful. Likewise, social groups which have defined their morality in this way have, throughout history, generally found themselves in serious conflicts with other similar groups, conflicts which have generally led to much grief and bloodshed.

The presence of these two columns of memory in the Second Degree suggests that as the individual climbing the Winding Staircase of consciousness begins to work at the level of the Middle Chamber or soul, the information stored in these archives becomes available to him. As he brings these long repressed memories into consciousness and examines them for what they are, he can permit the emotional charge they carry to dissipate. Then they become ordinary memories, available for reference, but no longer having the power to force or prevent behaviour. Instead, the individual achieves a greater freedom of action, for as he discards the compulsions and constraints of the super ego and the ego ideal he also discards the constraints of conventional morality. He then requires more fundamental criteria to guide his behaviour, which brings us to the consideration of the Working Tools of a Fellowcraft Freemason.

Working tools, which come in sets of three, are used in the practical application of the Rule of Three at the level of each degree. In contrast to the Apprentice's tools of action, the Fellowcraft's tools – the Square, the Level and the Plumb-rule – are tools of testing; and each tests against some absolute criterion. It is a characteristic which makes them well suited to represent standards of morality – the principal concern of the Second Degree. The Level measures against the criterion of horizontal; and in noting its passive, quiescent, sombre quality we can assign to it the psychological function of 'judgment'. The use of a single word to describe the function of the Level is obviously an oversimplification adopted for convenience; the tool actually represents a cluster of related concepts such as constraint, containment, confinement, rigour, discipline, defence, decisiveness and support. In a similar way the aspiring, vertical orientation of the Plumb-rule corresponds to the concepts of giving, forgiving, generosity, licence, and dissipation which can be summarized with the single quality of 'mercy'. From the nature of the ideas which we have associated with each tool we

Second Degree Working Tools

The fundamental issues of the Second Degree deal with individual morality. Therefore the Working Tools which must be identified and put to use within one's self test one's actions against the standards of Justice (the Level) and Mercy (the Plumb-rule). As always, the third tool, in this case the Square of Truth, defines the relationship between the other two.

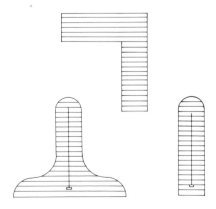

can see that neither is good or bad in itself. Each is what it is; and a life governed by an excess of either – unremitting discipline or unrestrained licence – is equally likely to produce serious difficulties. In practice, moral behaviour consists of maintaining the proper balance between the 'just' Level and the 'merciful' Plumb-rule; and the individual's capacity to maintain this balance consciously is represented by the third of the Working Tools, the Square, which in fact defines the relationship between the Level and the Plumb-rule.

In this way the Craft indicates that as a person matures he frees himself from the somewhat arbitrary psychological constraints imposed by his upbringing and his society and must look instead for the permissive and restraining standards of morality which reside within his own soul. These he must learn to work with, apply to his daily life, and keep in balance. The process of examining one's repressed memories can be, and generally is, difficult and painful. Usually there are excellent reasons why the material which must be examined has been excluded from consciousness, and recalling it often requires much personal courage. It is the hardest kind of work; it is a process to which the term 'Masonic Labour' can truly be applied; and it often requires the loving support of a close and trusted friend. It is in this context that we can begin to understand the bond of brotherly love and mutual trust which Freemasonry seeks to establish among its members.

By contrast, the actual experience of emerging from the restraint of the material stored in the two side pillars and taking possession of one's own standards of morality is usually one of joyful liberation. For the first time one is really free to choose; and a person who has worked at the level of the Fellowcraft and has come to terms with the compelling and constraining material in his unconscious can lay claim to genuine free will.

But there is genuine risk here too; free will is a truly dangerous thing. If the process of psychological growth is seen only as the discarding of compulsion and conventional standards of right and wrong and the replacing of them with one's personal standards of morality, the person working at the level of the Fellowcraft becomes an entirely free agent, responsible to no one but himself. Because such a situation can lead easily to self-indulgent and opportunistic behaviour it is at this point that Freemasonry and the schools of psychology based on the scientific paradigm of the twentieth century diverge sharply. From the viewpoint of Freemasonry there is much more to this process than simply the acquisition of free will – important though that is. There are other things to be considered, and these are introduced by a variety of symbols present in the Middle Chamber.

The most immediately relevant of these symbols is the second of the Immovable Jewels: the Perfect Ashlar. The Rough Ashlar, as we have seen, represented the Apprentice and alludes to his responsibility to shape and refine himself as an individual, but the Perfect Ashlar does *not* represent the Fellowcraft. It is made available in the Middle Chamber 'for the Craftsmen to try their tools on'. This important symbol reminds the individual that, although he is now free to make his own moral judgments, he is expected to calibrate his personal standards of morality against the standards provided for him by the Deity within his own soul. The idea seems to be that there is a body of psychological law which, in spite of appearance, is as stringent as the Laws of Physics. Historically these psychological laws have been found in the principles upon which codes of morality have been based; and this is one of the reasons why Masonry so frequently refers its members to the Scriptures. Of course, a human being is free to ignore the criteria of morality represented by the Perfect Ashlar, if he chooses; and the Craft outlines the implications of doing so by reference to the subject of Wages.

At the building of King Solomon's Temple the Fellowcraft Freemasons were said to have gone to the Middle Chamber to receive their wages which they did 'without scruple or diffidence', because they knew themselves to be entitled to them and because of 'the great reliance they placed in their employers'. Applying this to everyday activity suggests that the experiences of life are one's wages. The presence of the paymaster in the Middle Chamber of the soul indicates that one is given what one deserves not as a Divine reward or punishment, but by the working out of some principle which operates at the level of the soul. Furthermore, it says that the paymaster is fair, which implies first that the situation in which we find ourselves is the one we deserve (actually the working out of the natural process which we are called upon to observe and understand); and that if we wish to change our situation, we have the ability to do so by changing the way in which we live and act.

The idea is by no means original to the Craft; for Christian cultures it is contained in St Paul's dictum, 'As ye sow, so shall ye reap', and in the East it is found in the elaborate doctrines of karma. It is of fundamental importance as a warning to the newly passed Fellowcraft that he should restrain himself in the exercise of the freedom of choice which characterizes his level of consciousness. More important, it is the key to human freedom, since it emphasizes that the individual can and does determine his experience by exercising choice in each situation. It is the first step toward forgiving others, because a person who accepts responsibility for his own situation does not blame his problems on others. Thus wages represent not so much reward for merit and punishment for error, as harmonious experience for living within the psychological/moral law and difficult experience for trying to live outside it.

The last, and most important, of the symbols to be found in the Middle Chamber is the letter 'G' or, in some versions of the symbolism, an 'All Seeing Eye'. The letter 'G' is the initial of the Deity – not a representation of the Deity Itself, but the initial of Its name. Its presence in a place which symbolizes the soul conveys two ideas: first, that one's actions are 'observed', or 'recorded', or in some way incorporated into the fabric of existence with their inevitable consequences for good or ill. Second, it is a representation of the Blazing Star we saw at the top of Jacob's Ladder in the First Degree, but here we find it 'in the Centre of the building.' Its presence tells us that in operating at the level of one's soul, one can become aware of the presence of the Deity and orientate one's actions and aspirations toward It. With this capacity to sense the Divine presence the Fellowcraft is able to set aside the attitude of Faith which had guided him as an Apprentice and assume a positive outlook of Hope, for he is now able to glimpse his goal as he pursues the labours which will prepare him for the next step of his development.

The psychological processes of labour in the Second Degree are difficult and painful. Nonetheless, if the individual perseveres, he finds himself in the state of the mature Fellowcraft, in possession of himself, conscious of his standards of morality, and able to exercise his will freely. The ability to do that is the most fundamental objective of the Second Degree, for until a person is truly in possession of his will he cannot surrender it; and advancement to the Third Degree requires exactly that.

The Third Degree – Master Mason

The Master Mason's Degree is difficult to interpret because the ritual describes a psychological process which occurs only rarely in our society; one which, when it does occur, is so intensely personal that few who have experienced it are prepared to discuss it outside their intimate circle.

The Third Degree communicates a legend which is found, in one form or another, in almost every human culture. The legend has two aspects: the first is of a primordial disaster, a catastrophic event which results in profound loss and imposes great hardship on all mankind; the second alludes to the means by which the loss can be made good and the original, blissful, human state restored. Throughout Western Civilization the first aspect of this legend, that of primordial disaster, is embodied in the doctrine of the 'Fall of Man'. In our materialistic society the Book of Genesis is usually interpreted as a description of the Creation of the physical universe – in spite of the fact that such a position has become less tenable with almost every discovery in the physical sciences.

We have touched briefly on a mystical interpretation of this scripture in which Genesis I describes the 'creation' of the World of the Spirit and Genesis II the 'formation' of the soul and the World of the Psyche. In this context the 'Fall' and Adam's subsequent expulsion from Eden refers to the process by which members of the human race were first caused to incarnate by an act of Divine will. One of the consequences of this initial incarnation appears to be that human beings, having incarnated, have lost the ability to 'walk with God' and to be sustained by God directly. Instead, incarnate humanity is 'cut off', separate; and the incarnate individual must support himself by the 'sweat of his brow'. Framing that idea in contemporary terms, we might say that in its original state (that is, before the race first manifested on Earth) mankind was able to be conscious of, and communicate directly with, the Deity; and that some event connected with the process of incarnation disrupts that connection. In the Masonic treatment of this subject the events are described using the symbolism of Death.

The death described in the Third Degree is not the physical death which terminates our period of incarnation, but an individual psychological process that is in some ways analogous to physical death. The subject is introduced by re-enacting the murder of the Principal Architect, the junior of Three Grand Masters, at the building of King Solomon's Temple. The event is said to have occurred when the 'work [on the Temple] was nearly completed'; and as a result the 'secrets of a Master Mason' were lost, since they could be communicated only when all three Grand Masters were present and participating. The simplest and most obvious way to understand the legend is as an admonition always to be faithful to one's obligations; and that is certainly a valid interpretation. But when one reflects on the experience of the Degree, the grandeur and scope of the ceremony seem to overpower that simple explanation and invite our attention to the symbolic description of mankind's condition of separateness to which the story alludes.

Of course we are not entirely unfamiliar with the Architect who is slain. The symbolism of the Winding Stairs has introduced these Grand Masters and has already associated the Principal Architect with the Junior Warden/ Self. By this means we can relate the principles contained in the legend to the individual human being who is heir to the processes of the 'Fall'. If we consider the human being to be the 'Temple of God', then in one sense the building of that temple is nearly completed when the individual is about to be born. The person who is destined to occupy the infant body has a spirit, a soul and a Self; and he resides in Eden (the abode of innocent souls, not yet incarnate) in blissful contact with Divinity until the time for his birth arrives and his body (his 'coat of skin') is ready to receive him. In this context, the death of the Architect represents the event at the moment of birth when the Self (Junior Warden) is overwhelmed by the impact of confinement in his physical body and loses consciousness – particularly conscious contact with its soul and spirit and with Divinity. This 'death', or restriction of consciousness, reflects at the individual level the conscious separation from the Deity which the story of the 'Fall' describes for mankind. In the Masonic legend the Architect is said to be buried in a grave 'three feet East and three feet West [limited along the dimension of consciousness], three feet between North and South [limited in capacity for action and restraint] and five feet or more [the height of a man] in depth'. Furthermore, the legend implies that the blissful, Edenic state which preceded incarnation is possible only when all three Principal Officers – Self, soul and spirit – are operational; and in this sense it is clear why the 'secrets of a Master Mason' (the consciousness of the Upper Worlds) are lost.

The preceding paragraphs consider the first aspect of the Masonic legend, that of a primordial disaster; and offer an explanation as to how we come to be in our present, apparently isolated, situation. The second perspective on the legend speaks of how we can expect to repair the situation, and as we examine that second perspective it will become clear why the Lecture of the Third Degree says that 'to a complete knowledge of this Degree, few attain'. There is a second context in which a human being can be considered to be the Temple of God, and that is by recognizing that the psychological structure which we have seen the Mason building (or perhaps exploring) with such care is itself that 'Temple'. In this case the mature Fellowcraft whose condition was described above is, himself, the Temple which is almost finished; and the 'death' referred to in the legend is the psychological process by which the building will be brought to completion. It is a process of 'dying to one's self', and it is not entirely new to the Candidate for the Third Degree.

When he was initiated as an Apprentice the Candidate regarded himself as a physical being, albeit one who had an awareness that there 'was something more'. In the course of his development he will have 'died' to that idea and come to know himself to be fundamentally a psychological being, a human Self and soul, who occupies a body. The 'death' which faces the Candidate in the Third Degree will cause him to recognize that he is no more a psychological being than he is a physical one; but, rather, that he is a *spiritual* being who has both a soul and a body. The world 'recognize' is important. Most religious people *believe* that they have a spiritual essence. The psychological 'death' referred to in the Third Degree is concerned with the *experience* of that spiritual essence. Since that requires the death of the Candidate's Self (his psychological essence); and since his Self is his concept of his existence, that 'death' can be a very difficult and frightening process.

The ritual of the Third Degree, as it is conducted in the Lodge, simply describes the process of this 'death of the Self' in dramatic form; and in that way the ritual provides a sort of introduction to the subject. The actual event can occur only in people who are psychologically mature. Only a person who has assumed responsibility for his life, experienced the emergence of the Self, developed his own will, and is prepared to surrender it to the Deity is 'entitled to demand that last and greatest trial by which alone [he] can be admitted to the secrets of this [Master Mason's] Degree'. The wording of that quotation is important. The ritual is speaking of a psychological process; it will be difficult (a trial), the individual must initiate the process himself (he is entitled to demand it), and until this psychological process is allowed to occur the individual's development will cease (it is the sole means of advancement). The Lecture tells us that the real experience is accomplished 'by the help of God', and we may assume that it occurs when the Deity wills it. When it does occur, it comes, as do all Masonic initiations, in the context of 'the ordinary duties of [one's] station in life'. We can try to understand it by considering such a circumstance in general terms. Masons will recognize the situation as being parallel to the ritual of the Third Degree.

The individual finds himself in his ordinary life in a situation of great difficulty, but one for which he has been trained and with which he should be able to cope. As he works with the situation his abilities fail one by one. His analyses of the situation, seemingly correct, produce no useful answers; his actions, carried through on the basis of long experience, produce no beneficial result. Outside help is not available to him because his psychological situation prevents him from opening himself to those who could help him. Each time he turns to one of his carefully developed and trusted capabilities it betrays him. A means of escape from the situation presents itself, but he rejects it because it involves the violation of some moral principle which he is committed to uphold. Instead, he perseveres; the external circumstances worsen; and his situation continues to deteriorate. At last he turns to the 'East', to the place in his being which experience has taught him is the source of unfailing help in time of desperate need.

And it kills him.

What remains of him is buried in the rubble of the psychological Temple which he has built with such care.

We have already seen why this event occurs. The individual who conceives of himself as simply a 'soul' and believes there 'is something more' is as much caught up in the illusion of independent existence as he was when he thought of himself as simply a physical body. The trials which go to make up the individual's ordeal are the result of his own Masonic labours which have brought him to a situation in which he can no longer function within that illusion; and it is that illusory concept of himself, no longer adequate for the sort of life he must live, which dies. Just as the candidate in the ceremony does not remain long in the symbolic grave, so the period of disorientation in the real experience is not of long duration. The agency in the psyche which we have called the Worshipful Master emerges into consciousness to become the primary guiding principle within the individual who, in this new state, knows himself to be a Spiritual being possessing both a soul/Self and a body. The individual is raised from this grave of psychological rubble to find himself in a Master Mason's Lodge, in

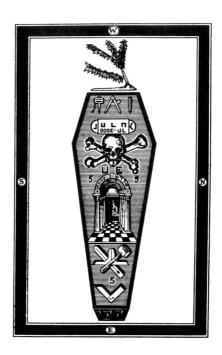

Third Degree Tracing Board

The Tracing Board of the Third Degree can be interpreted in two ways. First, like the other Boards, it shows a picture of the human individual. In this sense it indicates that the ordinary concept of human life is as death compared with the potential human capacity. Second, the view of the temple's interior suggests that through dying to one's concept of one's self one can realize that potential.

the Porchway Entrance to the Holy of Holies in the Temple which is his own being; and through its Veil he can glimpse the presence of Divinity. After this interior process has come to completion, the external situation which caused this psychological event seems easy to resolve or even to resolve itself; just as, in the legend, the murderers of the architect are brought to swift and certain justice. The process is summarized clearly by the Tracing Board of the Third Degree which points out that the way to this new interior state is through the experience of the death of one's Self.

In considering the previous Degrees we have understood the work to be accomplished at each level by examining one of the Three Immovable Jewels. The Rough Ashlar of the Apprentice indicated individual responsibility for one's self. The Perfect Ashlar in the Middle Chamber indicated the presence within each human soul of an internal absolute criterion against which the Fellowcraft must measure his morality. The Immovable Jewel which relates to the Master Mason is the Tracing Board; and, unlike the other Jewels, it does not relate to a single stone. Rather, as the drawing board on which designs are set out, it deals with the relationships between stones and with the whole of the larger structure to which they belong. That is to say, the concerns of the Master Mason are transpersonal and holistic.

This idea is communicated in another way. The Ornaments of a Master Mason's Lodge are the Porchway Entrance to the Holy of Holies (where the Master Masons' Lodge is said to meet), the Square Pavement of that porch, and the Dormer Window which illuminates the porch. This collection of symbols, and particularly their proximity to the place in the Temple where Divinity is said to reside, indicates that a Master Mason, in the sense that we are defining him, is a person who is conscious at a psychological level which relates to the World of the Spirit in the same way that our ordinary ego is conscious of the body and the physical world. He stands on the Square Pavement which is the same symbol of duality and separation which we saw in the First Degree, but in the light from the Dormer Window he sees that the apparently independent objects in the world are simply unique manifestations of the Divine Essence as it projects Itself into existence. In a very real sense the Master Mason is no more (and no less) than an individual whose responsibility it is to be conscious of that essential Unity, and to conduct 'the ordinary duties of his station in life' in that consciousness.

There is another way in which one can try to understand the level of consciousness represented by the Master Mason. As the Apprentice had tools of action, and the Fellowcraft tools of testing, so the Master Mason has Working Tools of design or creativity: the Pencil, the Skirrett and the Compasses.

The Pencil is the active tool. Just as when writing or drawing with a pencil the thoughts which reside in one's psyche 'change worlds', so to speak, at the pencil point and take the form of words or diagrams – the representations of the thoughts in the physical world – so the Pencil as the active tool of the Third Degree represents that point deep in the unconscious where material from the Spirit first enters the psyche and takes form in the mind – a phenomenon which we recognize as 'creativity' or even 'revelation'.

The Skirrett is a tool which, in practical use, is employed to constrain the pencil and to limit its motion; and that is exactly the role of the psychological function it represents. This function might be called 'understanding', a

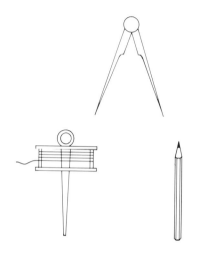

Third Degree Working Tools

The Working Tools of the Third Degree relate to the Spirit. They are tools of design, tools for planning and laying out the work. They refer to the capacity for creativity, the application of fundamental principles which put bounds on creativity, and the sense of proportion which keeps the two in balance.

definition which should perhaps be sharpened to convey the idea of Laws, Traditions and Fundamental Principles which come to be understood after careful, patient, exhaustive study and which can constrain and guide the enthusiasm of 'creativity'. Like all our psychological functions, these two need to be held consciously in balance.

The tool of consciousness which accomplishes this task is the Compasses. Known today as dividers, this is an instrument of proportion – the precise quality required to keep tradition and revelation, principle and creativity, in balance.

To get one last idea of the responsibilities which devolve on the Master Mason we note that he no longer aspires toward the East – his orientation has changed, as indicated by the cardinal points of the compass on the Third Degree Tracing Board. The Master Mason looks back toward the West from whence he has come in the attitude of the third of the Cardinal Virtues, Charity, which represents the frame of mind appropriate to the few who attain to this Degree in fact. On the Tracing Board of the First Degree, Charity stands on the highest of the principal rungs of Jacob's Ladder, largely in the part of the Board which represents the psyche, but with her head in the area representing the Spirit and illumined by the Glory of Divinity. She nurses a child, symbolizing the Master Mason's responsibility to nurture any who follow him.

These ideas give a picture of the Master Mason, a person who can be considered mature in the context of this developmental psychology we have derived from the symbols of Craft Freemasonry. He is one who stands in the light of the spirit, with his feet on the ground of the everyday world and recognizes, in fact, the single, integrated manifestation of Divine will through all the worlds. The development of such individuals is the purpose of the Craft. To find one's place in that single, integrated manifestation is a rich, fulfilling, deeply rewarding experience. It is like coming home.

> *To all poor and distressed Masons, wherever dispersed over the face of Earth and Water, wishing them a speedy relief from all their sufferings, and a safe return to their native country; should they so desire it.*

The Tyler's Toast

Freemasonry, like all mystical teachings, begins with the Deity as the centre and source of all things. The idea of God as a 'Great Architect' antedates speculative Freemasonry, as this painting of the Divine Being circumscribing the limits of creation indicates. (Page from the *Bible Moralisée*, c. 1250)

Although Freemasonry requires each of its Candidates to confirm his belief in God, it does not expand on the subject, but leaves religion and its practice to the individual Mason. As a result, men of all religious persuasions have been able to join in the study of Freemasonry's moral and philosophical principles. On this plate (*right*) from a Lodge in Madras, India, the cosmic rhythm of Shiva's dance holds the Universe in balance. (Brass plate, presented to his Lordship and Lady Cornwallis by the Lodge of Faith, Hope and Charity, No. 1285, Ootacumund-Nilgiris, India, 19 November 1986).

The more usual representation of the Deity in Craft symbolism is the Letter 'G', as on the plate *above*, which is decorated with the Three Great Lights of Masonry fashioned from butterfly wings. (20th-century Brazilian plate)

Overleaf Joshua commands the sun to stand still so that he might complete the 'battles of the Lord'; the story figures prominently in the Second Degree. However unlikely our contemporary knowledge suggests the astronomical event to have been, the 'battles of the Lord' are real enough. Masonic labour is interior work, work on the psyche; and the 'battles' are interior conflicts which occur on the battlefield of the soul when an individual undertakes the difficult task of knowing himself. No matter what name may be given to the process, a person in this situation may legitimately pray that the sun of consciousness be still and illuminate his psyche until he can bring the work to a successful conclusion. (John Martin, *Joshua Commands the Sun to Stand Still*, 19th-century English oil painting)

The operative masons of the medieval period are in many ways the predecessors of contemporary speculative Masons, and the work they have left behind — both the buildings themselves and the small carved figures with which they are often adorned — offers fascinating clues about their life and attitudes.

Out of the way places in the structures built by these early craftsmen are frequently decorated with carvings of masons themselves (*opposite*) as well as with fanciful demons (*above*). These 'imaginary' beings, which we would associate with psychological phenomena today, must have figured prominently in the life of a society whose interests were oriented toward the next world. (16th-century carvings from the flying buttresses, Cathedral of St John, S'Hertogenbosch, Holland)

I. PARAL. Cap. XXVIII. v. 11. 12. 13.
Exemplar Templi Salomoni traditum.

I. Buch der Chron. Cap. XXVIII. v. 11.12.13.
Salomon empfängt das Tempel-Modell.

G. Lichtensteger sculps.

Building in stone represented a large part of medieval activity (*opposite*). By the end of the 14th century, guilds of operative masons had developed a body of regulations which included a legendary history, professional and moral standards, formal procedures for admitting new members, and rules for training and discipline. Freemasonry derives much of its organizational structure from these guilds. ('The Building of 12 Churches by Count de Roussilon and His Wife', French manuscript, 1448)

King Solomon is said to have built his Temple at Jerusalem according to the plan for the Tabernacle which God had given to Moses in the desert (*left*). The plan of this archetypal Temple and the story surrounding its construction play an important part in the symbolism which communicates the teachings of Freemasonry. ('Solomon with Plans for the Temple', engraving from J.J. Scheuchzer's *Physica Sacra Iconibus Illustrata*, published Augsburg-Ulm, 1731)

The cathedrals, the grandest, most enduring and most exalted works of the medieval operative masons, are representations in stone of the Western metaphysical system. The fabric and form of the building reflect the structure of the relative Universe; and on the altar, if the Blessed Sacrament is reserved, the Deity is present at the building's central point through the miracle of the Eucharist. (Ripon Cathedral – the choir looking toward the west, c. 1160–70; J. de Heem, *Chalice with Host*, oil painting, 1648)

In the earliest days of speculative Freemasonry, the work of the Lodge consisted mainly of Lectures, and the symbols which illustrated them were sketched on the Lodge floor. This laborious process was replaced during the 18th century by Floor Cloths painted with the principal symbols (*above*). (Floor Cloth, c. 1804, on permanent loan from the Lodge of Hope, No. 433)

When Masonic rituals became the Craft's chief teaching method, the Cloth occupied floor space required for the working of the Degree. Cloths were gradually replaced by Tracing Boards – one for each Degree – which were freestanding, smaller, more durable and, when taken together, illustrated the same points. The Second Degree Board *opposite* shows the winding stairs which appear at the bottom centre of the Floor Cloth. (Tracing Board, Museum of the Grand Lodge of Ireland, designed by J. Harris, 1823)

In the frontispiece to the *Book of Constitutions*, 1784 (*below*), Truth, holding her mirror, illuminates the interior of Freemasons' Hall. She is accompanied by the Theological Virtues: Faith, Hope and Charity. To the 18th-century scholar, illustrations of this sort were more than pious wishes; they were technical drawings which gave information about psychological phenomena. This drawing suggests that Truth and her colleagues are to be found by pursuing the teachings of Freemasonry. (Allegorical plate drawn by G.B. Cipriani and P. Sandby and engraved by F. Bartolozzi and J. Fittler, *Book of Constitutions*, 1784)

The diagram on the Masonic apron given by General George Washington to General William S. Schuyler, a member of his staff, *c.* 1770 (*opposite*), is the same sort of technical drawing. In its treatment of the Three Columns it

summarizes the entire teaching of the Craft. Between the expansive and containing columns (symbolized by the sun and moon), which embrace all the paired opposites of the relative universe, the central, balancing column of human consciousness is pictured as a Temple of several storeys within which the individual has access to the Deity. (General Schuyler's apron, c. 1770)

Masonic Tracing Boards are training devices using symbols of the Renaissance classical revival assembled into integrated images. The First Degree Board (*above*) sets out the general Western metaphysical scheme and shows the place of the human individual within it.

The Second Degree Board (*centre*) is a symbolic representation of the individual in greater detail.

Here Jacob's Ladder has become a winding (spiral) stair leading to the interior of the Temple.

The Third Degree Board (*right*) alludes to a process, analogous to death, by which the individual can, if it be God's will, transcend the limitations of ordinary human life and realize a richer interior potential. (Wooden Tracing Boards, hand-painted by J. Bowring, 1819)

The representation of Jacob's Ladder as a spiral staircase is not restricted to Masonic symbolism. Blake depicted it so in his painting (*above*). (William Blake, *Jacob's Ladder*, watercolour, *c.* 1800).

The mountain *opposite*, with its spiral path forming seven tiers and set apart from the world by a portal, contains many of the elements of the Second Degree Tracing Board.

At each level scholars and philosophers receive instruction which originates from the Divine presence. ('Turris Sapientiae', Seven Liberal Arts, Florentine School, 15th century)

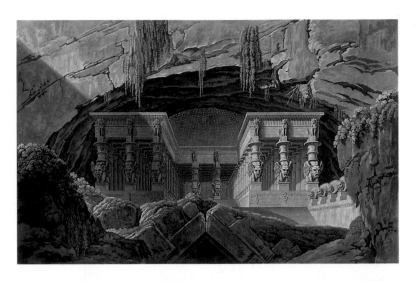

Participation in the ceremony of a Degree, such as the one being conducted in this Viennese Lodge in the 1780s (*right*) is a powerful experience through which the Mason can come to understand himself in ways which cannot be communicated by words. At the end of the 18th century, when the intellectual influence of the Enlightenment was still powerful and the generic relationship between Freemasonry and the Mysteries of antiquity was widely accepted, Mozart – said to be shown at the extreme right in this painting – incorporated the principles (though not the forms) of the Masonic Degrees into his opera *The Magic Flute*. Karl Friedrich Schinkel's sets (*above*). capture both the Egyptian idiom and the essential psychological orientation of the opera. (Meeting of Viennese Lodge, oil painting, 1780s; aquatints by Thiele after set designs by K.F. Schinkel for a production of *The Magic Flute* in Berlin, 1816)

This composition of a broken column, a weeping virgin and Time is a monument to Hiram Abiff, the principal Architect at the building of Solomon's Temple. The engraving (right), from an early-19th-century Masonic handbook explaining the emblems of Masonry, is one of the first instances of its appearance. In commemorating the death of Hiram Abiff, the monument symbolizes the condition of humankind after its expulsion from Eden. Humanity is represented by the virgin, bereaved by her loss, which is symbolized by the broken column of consciousness. Hiram's ashes are contained in the urn in her left hand. Hope of relief from her loss (re-establishment of the conscious connection with Deity) is promised by the sprig of acacia and by the workings of Time. (Engraving from J.L. Cross, *The True Masonic Chart, c.* 1808)

The composition is prominent in American Masonry, and in some parts of the Pacific. The bas-relief (right) shows a Japanese treatment of the subject. Its appearance among the familiar Masonic devices on a 19th-century Irish silver dish (opposite) is one of the few instances of its use in Europe. (Bas-relief by K. Nimori, in the entrance of the Tokyo Masonic Temple, late 20th century; Irish salver, 18in. [45cm] diameter, by J. and G. Angel, London, 1845)

The Craft's symbols point to the origin of its teachings and the perspective of its early members. The Arms of the Antient Grand Lodge (*above*) display the Man, the Eagle, the Lion and the Bull. Derived from Ezekiel, these symbols figure prominently in the Jewish mystical tradition, where they are archetypes of the inhabitants of the four worlds. (*Arms of the Antients*, oil on wood, mid-18th century)

The apron, originally an operative garment, is worn by all Freemasons as a mark of membership of the Order. Today the apron's design indicates a Brother's rank, but the early Masons decorated their aprons with the symbols of the Craft. Such aprons (*opposite top*) resemble today's Tracing Boards. In the 19th century special designs were worn to mourn the death of a Brother (*opposite below*). (Satin apron, English, *c.* 1800; skull apron, reversible, the Netherlands)

Here Masons engage in activities which suggest the breadth of the Craft's influence. George Washington and his Brethren (*right*) commemorate the Feast of St John, the patron saint of Masonry, at Christ Church, Philadelphia, in 1778. The French Brethren (*opposite below*) prepare to dine, probably after a Lodge meeting (*c*. 1875). In the painting *below*, Robert Burns is installed as Poet Laureate of Lodge Cannongate Killwinning No. 2 in Edinburgh. This room is the oldest Masonic Lodge room still in use. (*George Washington and Brethren*, mural by Allyn Cox; 'Repas des Franc-Maçons', French print, *c*. 1785; Stewart Watson, *The Inauguration of Robert Burns . . . ,* oil painting, 1846, presented to The Grand Lodge of Scotland in 1862)

Overleaf For nearly 60 years English Masons met in taverns and in the halls of City Livery Companies. The earliest Freemasons' Hall was built in Great Queen Street, London, in 1776. Some years later Sir John Soane, the first Grand Superintendent of Works for the United Grand Lodge of England, carried out modifications and extensions. Among them was this Lodge room, adjacent to the Temple in the 'New Hall' (*c*. 1828). Sir John Soane, *Masonic Hall*, exh. R.A. 1832)

· GEORGE W

AND BRETHREN IN SAINT JOHN'S DAY OBSERVANCE · CHRIST CHURCH PHILADELPHIA · 28 DECEMBER 1778 ·

Freemasonry can be seen as a doorway or entrance into the interior Temple. The closed door *above* draws attention to the need to knock before gaining admission, while the Jewel *opposite*, typical of the kind given to a Brother to commemorate some event in his Masonic career, places importance on the interior sanctuary. Both designs remind us that the entrance to the interior Temple lies on the middle way between the two side pillars, the paired opposites of duality. (Mosaic, latterly in the possession of Prins Frederik, Grand Master of the Grand Lodge of the Netherlands, 1816–1881; Irish Jewel, 2 × 2 × 2in. [5 × 5 × 5cm], early to mid-19th century, silver set with paste diamonds)

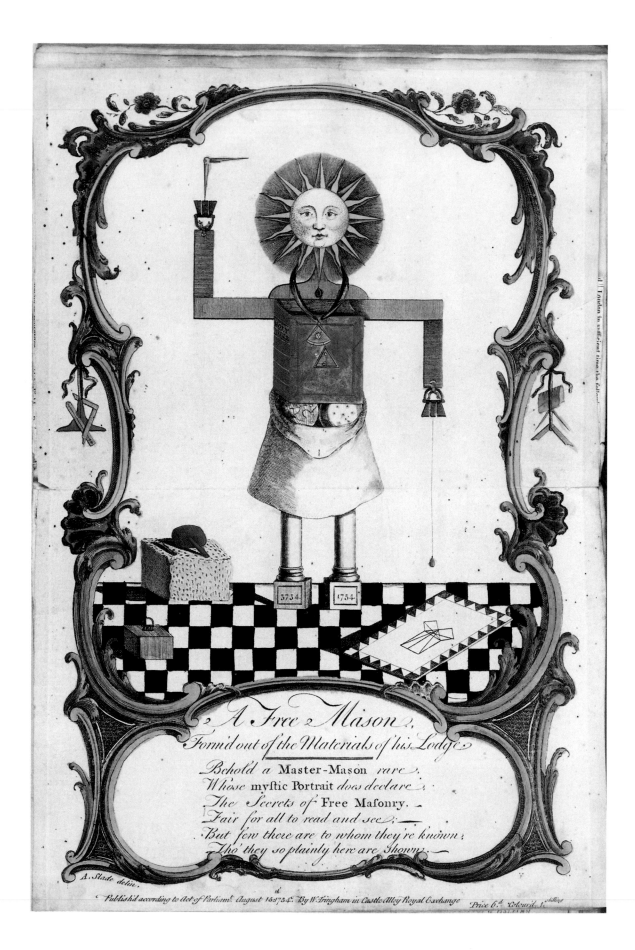

A Free Mason,
Form'd out of the Materials of his Lodge

Behold a Master-Mason rare,
Whose mystic Portrait does declare
The Secrets of Free Masonry,
Fair for all to read and see:
But few there are to whom they're known,
Tho' they so plainly here are Shown.

A. Slade delin.

Publish'd according to Act of Parliam.t August 16.t 1754. By W.t Tringham in Castle Alley Royal Exchange   Price 6.d Colour'd 1 shilling

This image is evocative of a Candidate's feelings when he first glimpses the interior of a Masonic Lodge. The various symbols of Freemasonry are drawn together, not to give material for analysis, but to provide a focus for quiet reflection and meditation on the philosophical principles of the Masonic system. (Drawing by Gideon Hausmann, 1971)

Rightly understood, a Masonic Lodge is an allegorical representation of the human psyche; so this 18th-century parody of 'A Freemason, Formed out of the Materials of his Lodge' does contain an element of truth. The 'materials of his Lodge' do, in fact, represent the elements of a Mason's being. To understand what that really means is the objective of Masonic labour. (Engraving, 1754)

The Egyptian Rite

Pharaoh Ouserei in masonic communication with the
High Grand Master disguised in Ibis mask. He has just
been invested with the Triangular masonic apron, surmounted
by the Apron of Serpents, emblem of Royalty & Symbl of The Fall.
He also grasps the Grand masonic Emblem, or Key of Life.

Origins – Early Theories

The drawing (*left*) goes too far in its speculation as to Freemasonry's origins, nevertheless, there has been much conjecture that Freemasonry comes to us directly from antiquity. Thus early-18th-century Masonic illustrations (*opposite below*) showed Masons constructing the cities of the ancient world. (Drawing, early 20th century; 'Workmen at Labour', from *Gründliche Nachricht von den Frey-Maurern*, Frankfurt, 1738)

In the late 18th and early 19th centuries many Europeans, Masons among them, found their way to the Middle East, where they discovered the relics of those cultures which had practised the Ancient Mysteries. Masons with a philosophical turn of mind recognized the similarities between their Order and the ancient traditions. The similar symbolism, some of which, like the ladder (*opposite far left*) from a Temple of Mithras, is shared with Masonry, encouraged the idea of Freemasonry's direct connection with those ancient rites. Egyptian motifs became a favoured Masonic decor which the print (*left*) and apron (*above*) reflect. (Mosaic with Mithraic grades, 3rd century AD; French print n.d.; French Master Mason's apron, c. 1800, showing busts of Napoleon and Cambacères, Duke of Parma, 2nd Consul of France, 1799)

Although there is evidence for a generic connection between the Craft and the Ancient Mysteries, there is no explanation of how the material might have been transmitted or how the tradition could remain hidden through the rigours of the Dark Ages and the probing of the Inquisition.

Origins – Recent Theories

Two themes in Freemasonry's symbolism give the best clues to its origin. First there is an 'Old Testament' orientation which stems from its many Biblical references such as the symbolic use of Solomon's Temple (*left*). The print of Jacob's Ladder *above left* conveys the mystical teaching of an interior avenue of communication between Heaven and the incarnate human being. Both the symbol and the concept are central to the Craft's teaching. (*King Solomon Shows Queen Sheba the Plans for the Temple which Are Held by His Architect Hiram*, oil painting, 1760; 'Jacob's Dream', engraving from *Works of John Milton*, London, 1794–1797)

Masonry also takes many of its symbols from Renaissance mystical tradition. Much of this material is to be found on the print *above right*, which alleges to set out the 'Mysteries' known only to a Mason. The frontispiece to *Chymical Collections*, 1650 (*right*), anticipates the Craft's Tracing Boards in its depiction of duality, represented by the male/sun and female/moon, and three columns. The column on the right exhibits active, warlike objects; that on the left, reflective intellectual ones; the central column reaches a Divine agency appearing from a cloud. ('The Mysteries that here are Shown', print, mid-18th century; frontispiece, *Chymical Collections*, London, 1650)

Late-18th-century Masonic diagrams (*opposite top left*) show similarities to alchemical prints of the same period (*opposite top right*). This Temple has columns named for those in front of King Solomon's Temple (J for Joachim, B for Boaz). (Reverse of miniature portrait of Frances Cornelia, wife of W. Bro. James Ames of Lodge Innocence and Morality, 1776; frontispiece to *Compass der Weisen*, 1779)

Fasciculus Chemicus:
OR
Chymical Collections.
EXPRESSING
The Ingreſs, Progreſs, and Egreſs,
of the Secret Hermetick Science,
out of the choiſeſt and moſt
Famous AUTHORS.

Collected and digeſted in ſuch an
order, that it may prove to the advantage,
not onely of the Beginners, but Proficients
of this high Art, by none hither-
to diſpoſed in this Method.

Whereunto is added, The *Arcanum* or
Grand Secret of Hermetick Philoſophy.

Both made Engliſh
By *James Haſolle*, Eſquire,
Qui eſt Mercuriophilus Anglicus.

*Our Magiſtry is begun and perfected, by onely one
thing; namely, Mercury.* Ventur. p.26.

London, Printed by *J.Fleſher* for Richard *Mynne*,
at the ſign of St. *Paul* in Little *Britain.* 1650.

Conflicting Authority: Formation of the United Grand Lodge

In 1717 four Lodges which had met from 'time immemorial' formed the first Grand Lodge in London. They adopted the Arms of the London Company of Masons (*left*) as the Arms of the Grand Lodge. Eight years later the number of constituent Lodges had grown to 64. They continued to grow (*below*) until by 1750 there were about 200 Lodges in England. Similar Grand Lodges were also established in Ireland, in Scotland and on the Continent. (Irish jewel showing Arms of the Moderns; 'Les Free-Massons', English print, 1736)

In 1717 there were other Lodges which had also met from time immemorial, some of which continued to work independently. In 1751 these independents formed a rival Grand Lodge, 'The Most Antient and Honourable Society of Free and Accepted Masons', choosing as their Arms the 'four living creatures' (lion, ox, man, eagle) which figure prominently in the vision of Ezekiel (top of the frontispiece *opposite*). Referring to themselves as the 'Antients', because they kept to old practices, they dubbed

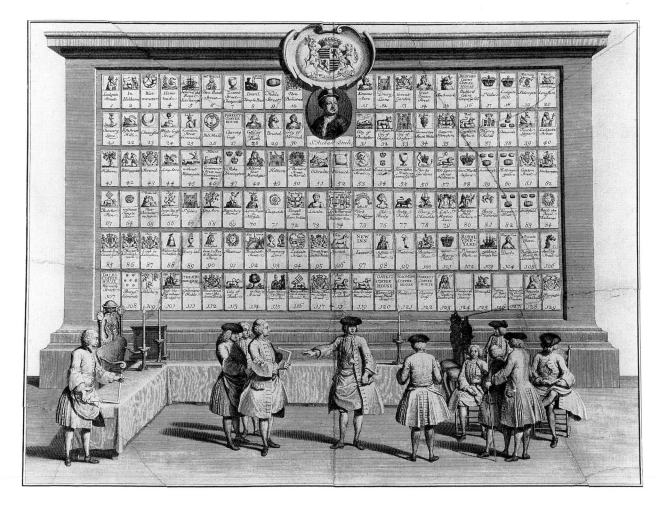

the older, original Grand Lodge 'Moderns' because of its innovations. The frontispiece to their book, *Ahiman Rezon*, 1764 (*below*) suggests that the 'Antients' are the real speculative Masons and the Moderns, members of the original Grand Lodge, are stone cutters. The 'Antients' received support from foreign Grand Lodges; in fact,

Masonry in Scotland, Ireland, on the Continent, and in the United Sates has generally tended to be 'Antient' Masonry. (Frontispiece: Arms of the Most Ancient and Honourable Fraternity of Free and Accepted Masons and the Arms of the Operative or Stone Masons, engraving, 1764, 2nd edition)

Efforts to reconcile the often bitter rivalry between these authorities succeeded in 1813 when the two Grand Lodges joined to form the United Grand Lodge of England. The Arms of the old rivals were impaled to form the Arms of the united body (*top*). The Arms of the 'Moderns' occupy the more important place, which is perhaps fair. Not only were they older, but during the union almost all the practices of the 'Antients' were adopted by the United Grand Lodge. In 1919, with the permission of H.M. George V, a border containing eight lions, passant, was added to mark the long association between the British Royal Family and the Order (*above*). (Arms of United Grand Lodge, 1813; Arms of United Grand Lodge, 1919)

The Ceremony of Making a FREE-MASON.

Evolution of the Ritual

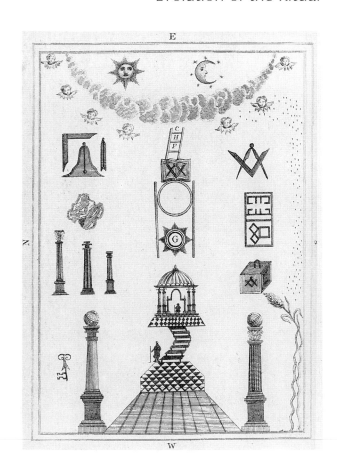

The first Masonic Lodges met in taverns, and conducted business during dinner. The principal form of instruction was the Lecture, a sort of catechism which embodies the elements of Western metaphysics as represented by Masonic symbols (*left*). Rituals conducted with the Brethren seated at table were very simple, as the print *above*, showing the initiation of a new Mason, suggests. (Frontispiece to *Masonic Miscellanies*, engraving by Stephen Jones, 1797; *The Ceremony of Making a Freemason*, print, mid–late 18th century)

After the founding of the Grand Lodge, emphasis changed from Lectures to more elaborate rituals (*opposite*), and by the early 18th century most Lodges were working a system which had two grades roughly comparable to the contemporary Apprentice's and Master's Degrees. By the 1730s many Lodges in England, France, Scotland and Sweden were conducting rituals containing three Degrees of the general form still in use today and by mid-century that practice was almost universal. (French prints, from *Les Costumes des Francs-Maçons dans leurs Assemblées, Principalement pour la Réception des Apprentifs et des Maîtres, c.1745*)

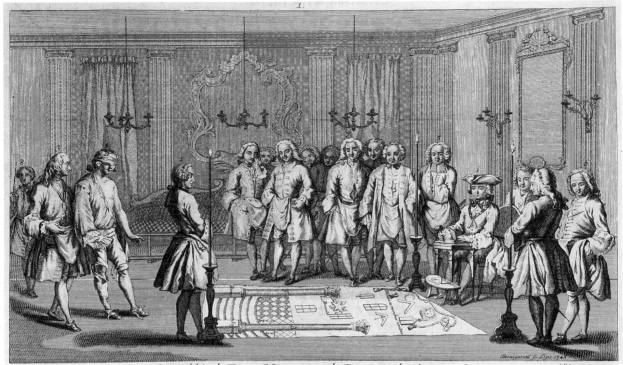

1. Le Grand-Maitre.
2. le p.er Surveillant.
3. le 2.e Surveillant.
4. le Recipiendaire.

Assemblée de Francs-Maçons pour la Reception des Apprentifs.
Entrée du Recipiendaire dans la Loge.
Dedié au tres Galant, tres sincere et tres veridique Frere profane Leonard Gabanon, Auteur du Catechisme des Francs-Maçons.
Dessiné par Madame la Marquise de ***, et Gravé par Mademoiselle ****.

5. l'Orateur.
6. le Secretaire.
7. le Tresorier.
8. le Frere Sentinelle.

1. Le Grand-Maitre.
2. l'Orateur.
3. le Secretaire.
4.5.6. Freres aux Rouleaux
de papier.
7. le p.er Surveillant.

Assemblée de Francs-Maçons pour la reception des Maitres.
Entrée du Recipiendaire dans la Loge.
Dedié au très Galant, très sincere et très veridique Frere profane Leonard Gabanon, Auteur du Catechisme des Francs-Maçons.

8. le 2.e Surveillant.
9. le Tresorier.
10. le Frere Sentinelle.
11. Recipiendaire entrant dans la Loge.
12. Recipiendaire aqui le Gr.d Maitre
n'a pas encore donné l'acollade.

The Temple as a Model of Man and the Universe

The idea that a temple should reflect the structure of both the universe and the human individual is probably 4000 years old; Moses built the Tabernacle in the Wilderness in that way (*right*). The area outside the fence represented the Physical World; the open court symbolized the Psychological World, the residence of the soul; within the Tabernacle itself (*right, bottom of picture*) was the Sanctuary, the World of the Spirit; in the innermost area, the Holy of Holies, the Deity was present. ('Tabernacle in the Wilderness/ Tabernacle Uncovered', print, London 1814)

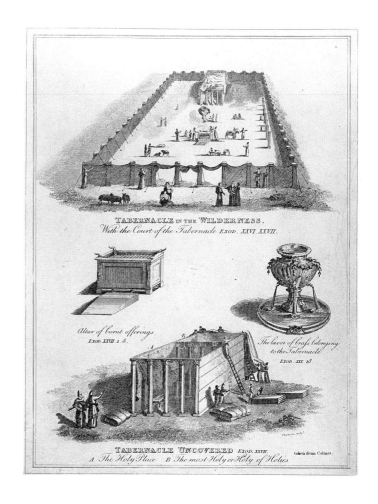

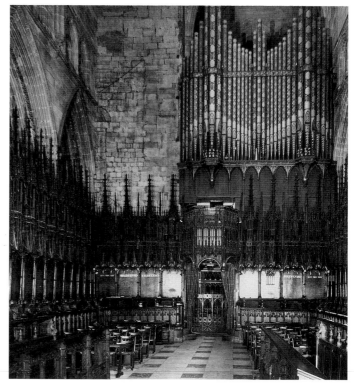

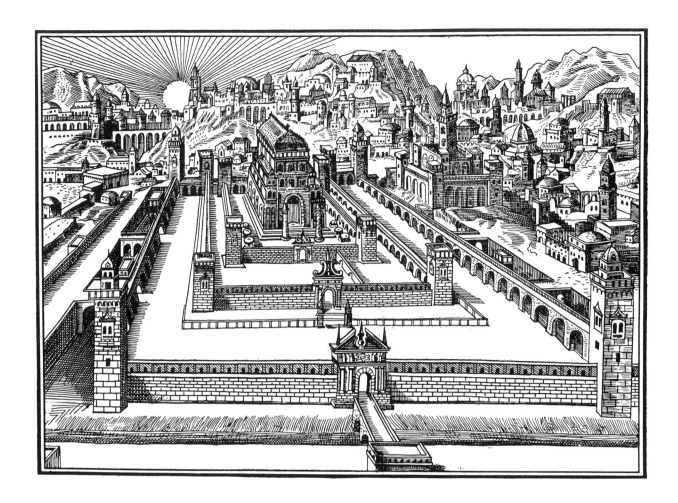

When Solomon built the Temple in Jerusalem (*above*) he followed the four-level plan of the Tabernacle. (Temple at Jerusalem, Passover Haggadah, Amsterdam, print engraved by Matthew Merian, 1695)

The same four levels are perpetuated in the Christian cathedral. The Physical World is represented by the Nave (*opposite left*): stone-built, cold and comfortless. The Choir (*opposite bottom right*) represents the World of the Psyche, the place of the soul: wooden, warm and intimate. The Sanctuary (*far left*) represents the World of the Spirit: splendid and brilliant. On the altar, the Deity is present in the Blessed Sacrament (*left*). (Lincoln Cathedral, *c.* 1220–35; Carlisle Cathedral, 1292–1324; Durham Cathedral, 1376–79; gold monstrance, Church of La Merced, Cuzco, Peru, 17th century)

Approaches to Masonic Labour

As there are three doors in the west wall of the Gothic cathedral (*left*), so there are three traditional ways to gain access to the 'temple' of the human interior: action, devotion, and contemplation. (West front of Strasbourg Cathedral, engraving, 19th century)

Since each way makes its own demands and has its own risks, European Masons provide an opportunity for applicants to take thought before joining the Order, which uses all three. In the 'Dunkel-kammer' or 'chambre de réflexion' (*below left*) the prospective Candidate sits soberly alone and writes his reasons for wishing to join the order. Only after his motives have been reviewed by the Brethren is he accepted as a Candidate. (Dunkel-kammer, 20th-century reconstruction of 18th-century room)

Ritual is the way of action (*right*). Its use in the dramas which constitute the Degrees make it the Craft's principal teaching method. By observing himself as he plays his role in the initiation of the Candidate, each Mason comes to know himself in the context of teaching a Brother. (*Adoption of Margrave Friedrich of Brandenburg-Bayreuth into Freemasonry*, illustration after a drawing by G. Hoffmann, 1740, and an anonymous oil painting in the collection of the Bayreuth Lodge 'Eleusis zur Verschwiegenheit')

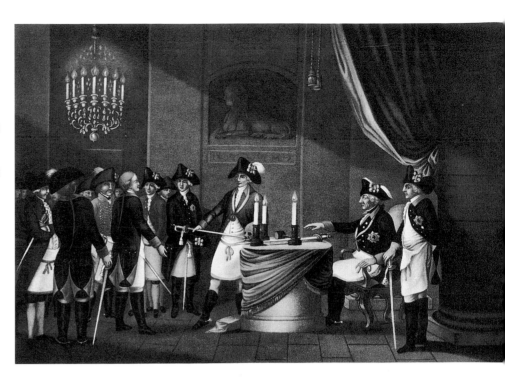

Devotion, the way of the heart, appeals most to persons with strong feelings. Followers of the way of devotion make extensive use of prayer, meditation, obedience and loving service. Freemasonry's devotional aspects show most clearly through its charitable works, such as teaching crafts to the blind (*below right*)

(Institute for the Education of the Blind, print, Amsterdam, 1808)

Contemplation is the way of the thinker. In following this way, the Mason becomes conversant with the symbols and the principles they represent; then he observes these principles functioning in his own experience. Discussion of the Tracing Board (*left*) is a means of understanding the symbolism. (Masonic Instruction, engraving, Vienna, 1791)

Levels of Consciousness

Freemasonry uses the ladder and the winding staircase as alternative representations of the central column of human consciousness in which role they symbolize an ascent through various levels along the East–West dimension. The Tracing Board *above* shows the stairs with seven steps ascending from West to East between the two complementary columns. The Masonic Lectures assign an Officer of the Lodge, represented here by their seven jewels (*opposite right*), to each of the seven levels. (Tracing board, engraved by F. Curtis and printed by F. Cole, 1801; Masonic jewels, n.d.)

The Lecture associates the three Grand Masters who presided at the building of Solomon's Temple (*left*) with the three uppermost steps, a reference which enables the Mason to relate the legend of the Third Degree, in which the three Grand Masters play a central role, to his own experience. (Chinese porcelain plate painted with scene of the building of Solomon's Temple, Chien Lung period, *c.* 1790)

The Lecture also associates one of the Seven Liberal Arts and Sciences (*above*) with each of the seven levels; and one of the Five Orders of Architecture (*opposite top right*) with

the five higher levels. In this way the Lecture directs the thoughtful Mason to a large body of Renaissance academic material which provides an insight into the nature of consciousness at each level. (Seven Liberal Arts; Vignola's Five Orders of Architecture, copperplate engraving, 1563)

LES BEAUX JOURS DE LA VIE.

Violence, Danger and Death

As the anti-Masonic print (*far left*) indicates, the Candidate for Masonry is confronted with danger as soon as he enters the Lodge. A poignard is indeed used (*left*), but in fact the Candidate is confronted not with one danger, but with two; and these dangers convey a warning found in all interior work (H. Daumier, *Reception of a French Freemason*, lithograph, 1846; silver dagger and sheath with Masonic symbols)

In ancient Greece the process of understanding the psyche was set out in the *Odyssey* which records the same dangers. During his voyage, Ulysses is required to sail between two monstrous creatures placed in such a way that to avoid one is to increase the risk from the other; Scylla and Charybdis (*right*) have become a metaphor for dangers which stand in that relationship. In the course of interior work it is sometimes tempting to rush ahead into an unknown, seemingly attractive, situation; alternatively, it is sometimes tempting to cling to the familiar when one should in fact move on. Properly interpreted, the experience of the two dangers warns the Candidate to be aware of these two tendencies and advises him to avoid them by a slow, steady, careful perseverance. (Scylla, engraved by T. Piroli from compositions by J. Flaxman, illustrating *The Odyssey of Homer*, 1793)

Harpies (*right*) have a special significance to Masons of the Second Degree, a stage at which much emotionally charged material is recovered from the unconscious. (Harpies, engraved by T. Piroli from compositions by J. Flaxman, illustrating *The Odyssey of Homer*, 1793)

Plan de la Loge du Maitre

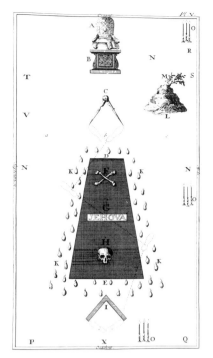

what dies is his previous concept of himself. (Print by Di Prinzio, Italy, 1980; *Assemblée de Francs-Maçons pour la Réception des Maîtres* [Reception of a Master Mason], print, c. 1750; *Plan de la Loge du Maître*, c. 1750; 'True' Plan of the Lodge for the Raising of a Master, from *L'Ordre des Francs-Maçons Trahi, et le Secret des Mopses Rélévé*, Amsterdam, 1745)

In the Masonic context, death is neither a danger nor the end of life; in fact, it is not physical death at all. It is a *psychological process*, analogous to physical death, which opens the way to an entirely new world. The Candidate recapitulates the process symbolically in the ritual (*right and below*). But as

the footprints on the Floor Cloths (*above left and above*) suggest, the Candidate does not remain in the grave, but *passes through* it from the level of the psyche (the Square) to the level of the spirit (the Compasses). When the event occurs, it occurs in the consciousness of the individual;

1. Le Grand Maitre.
2. le p.ᵉ Surveillant.
3. le 2.ᵉ Surveillant.
4. le Recipiendaire
   Couché sur le Cercueil.

Assemblée de Francs-Maçons pour la reception des Maîtres.
Le Recipiendaire est couché sur le Cercueil dessiné dans la Loge, le visage couvert d'un linge teint de Sang.
Et tous les assistans ayant tiré l'Epée lui presentant la pointe au Corps.

Dedié au très Galant, très sincere et très veridique Frère profane Leonard Gabanon, Autheur du Catechisme des Francs-Maçons

5.6.7. Recipiendaire
a qui le Grand
Maitre n'a pas
encore donné
l'acollade.

The FREE-MASON'S SURPRIZD or the SECRET DIS-COVERD.

A true tale from a Masons Lodge in Canterbury

The Chamber Maid Moll, a Girl very Moll happen to slip & ye ceiling broke thro With Phis white as a prong Masons ran, Comeal praying I, as as take warning by & the Masons may learn without touching Hoops,

lay hid in the Garret as sly as a Cat, & hung in ye posture you have in my View, & called up ye Parson his Clerke & the Town, The subject of this the Print & the Drole, That some of their Brothers are no Nincum poops,

To find out ye secret of Masons below, Which frighten'd ye Masons tha doing no evil, To lay ye poor Devil thus pendant above, To get a Secret which mere can be known, That Parson & Clerke with their sanctified faces,

Which no one can tell ye themselves do nothing, Who stoutly Cry'd out the Devil & Devil, Who, instead of old Nick, spy'd ye Temple of Love, By an unlucky slip she Dis-coverd her own, Had a Peep at Molls Rouser & just so ye Case is.

Printed for T. Wilkins in Rupert Street and Publish'd according to Act of Parliam.t Dec.r 26.1754.

Price 6.d Col.d

Anti-Masonry

The belief that Freemasons possess valuable secrets has undoubtedly tempted a great many eavesdroppers, like the chambermaid who fell through the ceiling (*above*), but in fact virtually nothing about Freemasonry is secret. The body of 'secret knowledge' which is revealed in stages to a Candidate is an allegorical reference to the unconscious; and the secrets of Freemasonry are the secrets found in the unconscious of each person. They are discovered by each individual, Mason or not, as he comes to know himself. (*The Freemasons surprizd*, engraving 1754)

Freemasonry sometimes attracts the attention of satirists, like Hogarth, who, in his engraving *Night* (*right*), showed a Freemason returning drunk from a Lodge meeting; or like Lawson Wood, who casts 'Gran-Pop' (a chimpanzee) as a Mason giving instruction to three piglets (*right below*). (William Hogarth, *Night*, print from the *Times of Day* series, 1738; cartoon by Lawson Wood, 1935)

However, the Craft is sometimes attacked for reasons which are genuinely sinister (*opposite below* and *below*). (The Work of the Freemasons, published by the Belgian Anti-Masonic League, May 1912; Die Überstaatlichen Mächte [Powers which are beyond state control], anti-Masonic/Christian/semitic cartoon published by the Nazis, 1930)

Die Überstaatlichen Mächte

"GRAN-POP" SERIES

GRAN'POP DISCLOSES THE SECRETS OF MASONRY.

JOSÉPHINE.

«Mes frères et mes sœurs,—dit l'aimable compagne
Du grand Napoléon, cet autre Charlemagne:—
«Mon époux a dit vrai, l'exemple, les leçons
«Des vertus, de l'honneur, viennent des Francs-Maçons.

(Paroles de l'Impératrice Joséphine, à la fête d'adoption des Francs-Chevaliers à Strasbourg en 1805.)

DECHEVAUX-DUMESNIL,
Rédacteur en chef du Journal le FRANC-MAÇON.
58, Quai des Orfèvres, à Paris.

Women and Masonry

'Adoptive Masonry' was a phenomenon of the mid-to-late 17th century. A Lodge of Adoption was conducted by a regular Masonic Lodge which held special meetings in the course of which women were admitted into the Lodge and participated in elaborate, courtly, quasi-Masonic ritual (*opposite top left*). Such Lodges were particularly successful in France, where there was a revival of Adoptive Masonry after the Revolution which continued in the next century (*opposite below*). Empress Josephine herself served as Grand Maîtresse du Loge d'Adoption Sainte-Caroline (*opposite top right*). (Reception of a Lady into a Lodge of Adoption, French print, 18th century; *First Degree Initiation*, French watercolour, early 19th century; Josephine, lithograph by C. Delamarre, French, 19th century)

The Order of Mopes derived its name from the pug dog, which was thought to exemplify the 'fidelity and attachment' between members. A Catholic Order accepting both men

PLAN DE LA LOGE DES MOPES

a. Orient.
b. Midi.
c. Occident.
d. Septentrion.
e.e.e.e. Les quatre Lumières.
f. Mopse, ou Doguin.
g. Fidelité.
h. Amitié.
i. Porte qui conduit au Palais de l'Amour.
k. Palais de l'Amour.
l. Cheminée de l'Eternité.
m. Sincerité.
n. Constance.
o.o.o.o. Cœurs semés

POUR LA RECEPTION DES FEMMES.

pp. Cordon du plaisir, qui lie les Cœurs.
q. Vase de la Raison.
r.r.r.r. Divers Symboles de l'Amitié.
s. Maitre de la Loge, ou Grand Mopse, assis devant la Table.
t.t. Surveillans.
n. Etrangers et Etrangères.
x. Officiers et Officières.
y.y.y.y. Frères et Sœurs, placés indifferemment.
z. Trape que l'on pratique dans quelques Loges, et sur laquelle on place le Recipiendaire, pour l'élever en l'air, tandis qu'il a les yeux bandés.

and women, it was founded in Vienna in competition to Freemasonry after the anti-Masonic Papal Bull in 1738 and may have been established by Augustus I, Elector of Saxony. The toy dog *above*, particularly in a ritual of Masonic-like setting, suggests Mopes; and the lady in the porcelain group (*left*) wears the sash of the Order. It enjoyed considerable popularity on the Continent, but did not survive the 18th century. (Reception of a Lady into the Order of Mopes, French print, 1745; Viennese porcelain group after model by Kaendler, late 18th century)

Masonry Universal

This jewel (*left*), with its Zoroastrian conception of the Deity as Ahura-Mazda, makes reference to the Persian heritage of the Grand Lodge of Iran, the consecration of which, in 1969, illustrates the breadth of Freemasonry's appeal. (Jewel commemorating the foundation and consecration of the Grand Lodge of Iran, 1 March 1969)

In its earliest years the Craft was probably an exclusively Christian organization simply because of the demographic structure of 17th-century England; its non-sectarian view of the Supreme Being was perhaps essential, given the fierce religious intolerance common among Christians of that period. Nonetheless, such a view certainly admits the possibility of non-Christian membership, and records as early as 1732 reveal that a Jewish Mason was Master of his Lodge which met at the Rose Tavern in Cheapside, London. This rigorously non-sectarian view of the Deity certainly assisted Freemasonry's expansion outside England, as is illustrated by mid-18th-century documents. The summons *above*, used to announce a meeting of the Lodge, is German, and the certificate of membership in the 'Loge le Parfait Silence' in Lyon (*left*) required printing in three languages: French, Italian and English. (Summons to attend Viennese Masonic Lodge, engraving by J. Schmutzer, 1784; membership certificate, *c.* 1760)

The Craft's philosophical orientation epitomized the values of the Enlightenment, and it attracted educated men such as the Abyssinian

Angelo Soliman (*below*), a member of the household of the Duke of Lobkowitz, and prominent intellectuals such as Voltaire (*below left*) and the German dramatist Lessing (*above*). (Λ. Soliman, 1760; bust of Voltaire by Houdon, 1781; O. May, *Portrait of Lessing*, 1729–1781, oil painting)

By the mid-19th century, Freemasonry claimed members from almost every country and culture; the French print (*left*), 'La Maçonnerie secourant l'Humanité', suggests the broad scope of its interests and charitable concerns. Some Masons were notable people. Emir Abd-el-Kader (*bottom centre*), Arabian by birth, was a French Mason, a dedicated Muslim, and a leader of great personal integrity. (French print, mid-19th century; Emir Abd-el-Kader, c. 1865)

A Nation under God

A great many American patriots of the revolutionary period were Masons, including Benjamin Franklin (*above*) and George Washington (*right*). (Benjamin Franklin, engraving by J. Thomson, late 18th century; George Washington in Masonic regalia, engraving by Currier and Ives, 1868)

The Great Seal of the United States, which appears on the one dollar bill, exhibits many principles familiar to Freemasons. At the top of the obverse side (*right*) is the Glory, a heraldic representation of the Deity, and beneath it is the Eagle, a symbol of the spirit. At this first remove from the Deity is the symbol of paired opposites: the Laurel of Peace and the Arrows of War. The Eagle carries the 'form' of the Nation represented by its Arms. The four levels are completed on the reverse of the Seal (*left*), where the motto says that this nation, which rises from a broad, diverse base (the pyramid) to the single Divine centre (the eye) which is its source, is to be a 'New Secular Order'. (The Great Seal of the United States)

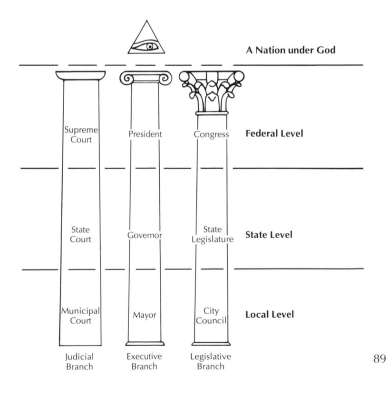

George Washington's apron (*above*), like many aprons of its period, resembles a Tracing Board. One of the distinctive characteristics of the American Constitution is the 'separation of powers' among the three mutually checking and balancing branches of the government, Legislative (expansive), Judicial (containing) and Executive (coordinating); we have met this idea already in the Three Columns on the Tracing Board (*above right*). This government of mutually balancing agencies (*right*) operates in a hierarchy parallel to that on the Great Seal. From local, through State, to Federal government, the structure is conceived as existing 'under God'. (Print, made from cloth reproduction of George Washington's original apron; Tracing Board, 1801; Masonic drawing, 1991)

It is not unreasonable to believe that the framers of the Constitution, serious thinkers of their time, designed it to reflect their understanding of Natural Law. Nor is it unreasonable to think that they might design a government which, like the cathedrals of an earlier age, provides instruction to the individual citizen about his own nature.

89

Allegations of 'secret organization' notwithstanding, Freemasonry conceals neither its existence nor its activities. In the late 18th and early 19th centuries Masonic symbols enjoyed wide popularity as motifs for decorative art; and personal and household objects often appeared with Masonic designs. Masonic decoration achieved greatest popularity in the United States where it was closely associated with the development of American patriotic symbols. The chest of drawers *above left* with marquetry Masonic design is American, dating from 1800, and typical of the work of the period. (Tiered chest of drawers, wood, M.1908.19)

Masons travelling throughout the world commissioned local craftsmen to make objects with similar decoration (*left centre and bottom*). (Japanese lacquer box, mid-19th century; Chinese punch bowl, pre-1812)

Throughout the 19th and early 20th centuries public functions such as the Oxford Commemoration Ball in 1863

(*above*), at which Masons appeared in their regalia, were by no means uncommon; engraved invitations (*opposite top right*) announced Masonic events. Public Masonic ceremonies frequently involved civic or community activities; in 1921 the Lord Bishop of Willesden, in his capacity as Past Grand Chaplain, laid the cornerstone of St Michael and All Angels Church in Mill Hill, London, in a ceremony which attracted considerable public attention (*right*). (Oxford Commemoration Ball, given to the Prince and Princess of Wales in the New Corn Exchange on 4 July by the Apollo University Lodge, *Illustrated London News*, 1863; Bishop of Willesden laying cornerstone, 1921)

Since World War II taste in entertainment has changed, and public exercises of the sort in which Masons used to participate are rarer. This change, together with a reserve which Masons adopted in the 1930s as a result of·hostile publicity, has given late-20th-century Freemasonry an undeserved reputation for secrecy.

National Style

Although Freemasonry maintains a single set of principles, there is no single authoritative, international Masonic organization. Perhaps nowhere is this more plain than in the architectural design of Masonic Lodges and buildings. The design of the gates guarding the entrance to the Temple of the Grand Orient de France (*above left*) displays the style and elegance characteristic of that country. 'Marianne Maçonnique' (*above*) is prominent in French Masonic symbolism and reflects the emphasis which many members of the French Craft place on their social responsibilities. (French gate, 1910; bust of Marianne Maçonnique by J. France, end 19th century)

The Grand Temple of the Grand Lodge of Ireland (*left*) was built in the mid-19th century. It typifies British, and to some extent European, architecture of that period. (Grand Temple Room, Dublin, Ireland)

The British style contrasts markedly with the Blue Lodge Hall in the Tokyo Masonic Building (*right*), which illustrates the remarkable Japanese capacity for understanding and integration. Traditional Masonic symbolism fits very comfortably in the surroundings of contemporary Eastern architecture. (Blue Lodge Hall, Tokyo Masonic Building, after 1950)

Lodges built on the Continent of Europe since World War II often have the austerity exhibited by the Masonic Temple in Eindhoven, the Netherlands (*right below*). The plan *below*, for Sint Ledewijk Lodge in Nijmegen, suggests the use of sacred geometry by philosophically inclined Masons. (Masonic Temple, Eindhoven, 1955; plan for Lodge Sint Ledewijk, Nijmegen, the Netherlands)

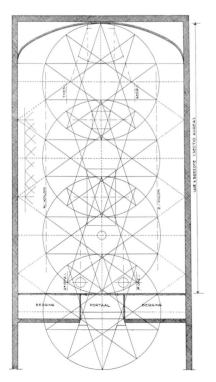

Charity

The admonition to be charitable comes early in a Mason's career, in the ceremony of his initiation. Though today's Masons tend to support such established charities as Britain's Royal National Lifeboat Institution (*left*), in the

18th and early 19th centuries charitable activities were largely *ad hoc* donations (*above*). The French print *left* commemorates a venture by French Freemasons to relieve suffering during the difficult winter of 1789. (*The Duchess of Kent* lifeboat, purchased by Masonic subscription, 1982; *Appeal for Charity*, engraving by J.G. Schadow, 1832; En Mémoires de Secours . . ., engraving by F. Louvion)

CITOYENS DE L'UNIVERS LA BIENFAISANCE LES UNIT TOUS D'UN POLE A L'AUTRE.

En Mémoire des secours donnés aux
Malheureux, par les F.F. Maçons, pendant
le Rigoureux Hyver de l'année 5789.

Le bien qu'on a fait la Veille,
Fait le bonheur du lendemain.

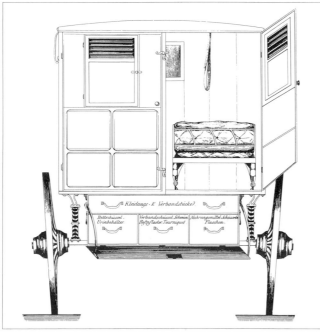

Masons also funded ambulance wagons (*left*) used in the Swiss Sonderbund war of 1847. (Ambulance wagon, 1848, collection of Lodge 'Modestia cum Libertate', Zürich)

The end of the 18th century saw the establishment of charitable institutions. Although some may seem harsh when evaluated by contemporary standards, they represented a great social advance at the time. The Royal Masonic School for Girls (*above*), known in 1790 as The Masonic Girls' School, is typical of Masonic institutions founded in Ireland, Britain, on the Continent and in the United States. (Print representing the distinguishing characteristic of Masonry, Charity, exerted on proper objects, engraved by Bro. Bartolozzi, R.A., Engraver to His Majesty, 1802)

SOURCES

Allen, Paul M., and Pietzner, Carlo, eds., *A Christian Rosenkreutz Anthology*, New York, 1969

Campbell, Joseph, *Hero with a Thousand Faces*, Princeton, N.J., 1968

——, *The Masks of God*, New York, 1970

Campbell, Joseph, and Moyers, Bill, *The Power of Myth*, ed. Betty Sue Flowers, New York, 1988

Campbell, Joseph, ed., *The Portable Jung*, New York, 1971

Dyer, Colin, *Symbolism in Craft Freemasonry*, London, 1976

Fletcher, Banister, *A History of Architecture*, New York, 1946

Flon, C., ed., *Le Grand Atlas de l'architecture mondiale*, Paris, 1981

French, Peter J., *John Dee*, London, 1972

Freud, Sigmund, *Introductory Lectures, The Standard Edition of the Complete Psychological Writings*, Vols. XV and XVI, London, 1953–74

——, *Outline of Psychoanalysis, The Standard Edition of the Complete Psychological Writings*, Vol. XXIII, London, 1953–74

Halevi, Z'ev ben Shimon, *A Kabbalistic Universe*, London, 1977

Hall, Calvin S., *A Primer of Freudian Psychology*, New York, 1954

Hall, C.S., and Nordby, V.J., *A Primer of Jungian Psychology*, New York, 1973

Hamill, John, *The Craft*, Wellingborough, Northants, 1986

Hanrath, John J., Pott, P.H., Croiset van Uchelen, B., *De Beoefening der Koninklijke Kunst in Nederland*, The Hague, 1971

Jacobs, J., ed., *The Horizon Book of Great Cathedrals*, New York, 1968

Jones, Bernard E., *Freemasons' Guide and Compendium*, London, 1950

Jung, C.G., *Seven Sermons to the Dead*, London, 1925

——, *Man and His Symbols*, New York, 1964

Kettlewell, G.D., *Mopses*, Blandford Forum, Dorset, 1902

Klossowski de Rola, S., *The Golden Game*, London, 1988

Lester, R.P., *Look to the East!*, Hackensack, N.J., 1969

Linder, E.J., *Die Königliche Kunst im Bild*, Graz, 1976

MacNulty, W. Kirk, *The Way of the Craftsman*, London, 1988

Morata, R., *La Franc-Maçonnerie*, Paris, n.d.

Pereau, Abbé, *L'Ordre des Franc-Maçons Trahi, et le Secret des Mopes Révélé*, Amsterdam, 1745

Rait, Robert S., *Life in the Medieval University*, London, 1912

Rosenau, Helen, *Vision of the Temple*, London, 1979

United Grand Lodge of England, *Masonic Yearbook for 1988–9*, London, 1988

——, *Constitutions of the Antient Fraternity of Free and Accepted Masons*, London, 1989

Valmy, M., *Die Freimaurer*, Munich, 1988

Voorhis, Harold van B., *Eastern Star: The Evolution from a Rite to an Order*, New York, 1938

Yates, Frances A., *Giordano Bruno and the Hermetic Tradition*, London, 1964

——, *The Rosicrucian Enlightenment*, New York, 1972

——, *The Occult Philosophy in the Elizabethan Age*, London, 1979

——, *The Art of Memory*, London, 1984

ACKNOWLEDGMENTS

t = top,   c = centre,   b = bottom,   l = left, r = right

Objects reproduced in the plates, courtesy of:

Alexandria, Virginia, Property of Alexandria-Washington Lodge No. 22, A.F. & A.M. (photo Arthur W. Pierson) 47, Courtesy of the George Washington Masonic National Memorial Association 59t; **Chantilly**, Musée Condé (photo Giraudon) 51; **Dublin**, Grand Lodge of A.F. & A. Masons of Ireland 45, 54, 63, 64; **Edinburgh**, The Grand Lodge of Antient, Free & Accepted Masons of Scotland 58; **The Hague**, Courtesy of Freemasons' Hall 38 (photo Marten F.J. Coppens), 59b, 62 (photo Rob Mostert); photo **A.F. Kersting** 42; **London**, British Museum 50, By Courtesy of the Trustees of Sir John Soane's Museum 60–61, Board of General Purposes of the United Grand Lodge of England 4, 35, 36–37, 44, 46, 48–49, 55t, 56, 57t, 57b, 65; **Paris**, Musée du Grand Orient de France et de la Franc-Maçonnerie Européenne, 34; photo **Max Seidel** 39; **Tokyo**, Grand Lodge of Free & Accepted Masons of Japan 55b; photos **Eileen Tweedy**, 4, 35, 44, 46, 48–49, 55t, 56, 57t, 57b, 65; **Vienna**, Historisches Museum der Stadt Wien 53, Kunst-historisches Museum 43, Osterreichische Nationalbibliothek 33, 41, 52t, 52b

Photographs supplied by:

Bayreuth, Deutsches Freimaurer Museum 68b; **Berlin**, Archiv für Kunst und Geschichte 87tr; **Cuzco**, Church of La Merced (photo Abraham Guillen) 75br; **Dublin**, Grand Lodge of A.F. & A. Masons of Ireland 70t, 92b; **The Hague**, Courtesy of Freemasons' Hall 77br, 93bl, 93br; **Jerusalem**, Jewish National University Library 75t; photos **A.F. Kersting** 74bl, 74br, 75bl; **London**, British Museum 83t, 90r, Board of General Purposes of the United Grand Lodge of England 66t, 67t, 68tr, 69tl, 69tr, 71tr, 71cr, 72t, 72b, 73t, 73b, 74t, 77t, 78b, 79l, 79r (photo Middlesex Lodge No. 143), 80tl, 81tl, 81tr, 81b, 82t, 82b, 83br, 85t, 85b, 86tl, 88tl, 89tr, 91t, 91b, 94b, 95t, Victoria & Albert Museum 70b, 87bl; **Paris**, Bibliothèque Nationale, 76t, 87bc, Musée du Grand Orient de France et de la Franc-Maçonnerie Européenne, 67b, 84tr, 84b, 86b, 92tr, 92tl; **Philadelphia**, Collections of the Grand Lodge of Pennsylvania on deposit with the Masonic Library & Museum of Pennsylvania 71l, 80tr, 87tl, 88tr, 89tl, 90tl, 90cl, 90bl; **Rosenau**, Osterreichisches Freimaurer Museum (photo Günther von Voith-enberg, Munich) 76b; **Royal National Lifeboat Institution** 94tl; **Soprintendenza di Roma** (Scavi di Ostia) 66l; **Tokyo**, Grand Lodge of Free & Accepted Masons of Japan 93t; photos **Eileen Tweedy** 67t, 69tl, 85b, 86tl, 95t; **Vienna**, Albertina 86tr, Osterreichische Nationalbibliothek 87br; **Zurich**, Courtesy of Lodge 'Modestia cum Libertate' 95b

The following books were also used:

G. Barozzi da Vignola, *Regola delli Cinque Ordini d'Architettura*, 1607, 78tr; *Die Freymaurer im Fischbein-Rocke*, Frankfurt und Leipzig 1771, 84tl; *Gründliche Nachricht von den Frey Maurern*, Frankfurt 1738, 66b; James Hasolle, *Fasciculus Chemicus or Chymical Collections*, London 1650, 69b; *Illustrated London News*, July 1863, 91t; *The Odyssey of Homer*, engraved by Thomas Piroli from compositions by John Flaxman, sculptor, Rome 1793, 80c, 80b; Pereau, Abbé, *L'Ordre des Francs-Maçons Trahi, et le Secret des Mopes Rélévé*, Amsterdam 1745, 81tr; Johann Jakob Scheuchzer, *Physica Sacra iconibus illustrata*, Augsburg-Ulm 1731, 40; *Der Verklärte Freimaurer*, Vienna 1791, 77bl